Forty-Six Meditations for the Thinking Chief Executive

The CEO Handbook - Volume One

Dr. Earl R. Smith II

Raven Press

Comments On The Book

The book is great! It gives perspectives that are not only enlightening but flow of the book stimulates the thought process associated with building a truly successful business. It is direct for those willing to open their minds and understand that they are not the single greatest business authority. This book provides a refreshing view of the dual process involved between the CEO and the expert on how to take a company to the next level – the level of success!

~~~~~~

What a great read! You portrayed the process of achieving excellence in an organization with wonderful detail. From the challenge to the resolution, I found myself identifying strongly with the efforts. The roll out of the material was well ordered and an easy read. I could empathize and relate strongly from the facilitation I've done over the years. I'm encouraged by the language and style of your efforts and your ability to relate the details concisely noting several key philosophies we have in common, especially the preparation, strategic and holistic approaches. It really is challenging to get people out of their boxes, even when popping the lid off will catapult their success. I absolutely love the work.

~~~~~~

Over the five years that I have worked with Dr. Smith I have found him to be a visionary in the areas of technology assessment and organizational change. Whether serving as a senior strategic advisor or chairman of the board, he brings real value to any relationship and is always an agent for growth. He has, on many occasions, provided me with very helpful and insightful assessments of my portfolio companies and their management. I consider him a trusted and reliable advisor and look forward to working with him in the future. This book is a reflection of his understanding and ability to make contributions.

~~~~~~

CEO Handbook "You should charge more for this book! It's pure gold. I reread a chapter every evening & learn more."

~~~~~~

"Many thanks Doc for this book. Volume One of the CEO Handbook is a great reference. I go back to it regularly."

~~~~~~

"What a great book. Thanks Doc. I wish I had it when I started my company. Glad to have it now."

~~~~~~

"Dr. Smith focuses on a positive outlook, he definitely drives you to face hard truths and deal with them head-on."

~~~~~~

"Dr. Smith is a pragmatic mentor who helps you explore and build on your innate strengths and passions."

~~~~~~

"Dr Smith sets the bar high, has clear expectations, and does not let you rest on your laurels."

~~~~~~

"My work with Dr. Smith has been nothing less than a transformation of my professional life."

~~~~~~

"Dr. Smith has shown me how to leverage my experiences to set a course for my career with a disciplined approach."

~~~~~~

"Dr. Smith focuses on actions, setting metrics, giving advice and letting you take the reins of your own destiny."

~~~~~~

"There's no substitute for doing. Writing about what you haven't mastered is like thinking about being alive."

Introduction

During my business career, I have built six companies, started two non-profit funds and worked with dozens of senior executives - helping them to build their companies. As I look back over those years, I am struck by the diversity of my experiences and the knowledge that I have accumulated. As one of my early mentors was fond of observing, "There is no substitute for having done a thing. Writing about what you haven't demonstrated mastery of is like thinking about being alive. It just isn't the same thing."

As with any such undertaking, an author owes his readers a description of his background and experience. You have a right to know who it is who writes and the basis for his presumption.

My experience includes designing and organizing companies, business/technology management, team building, strategic alliances, negotiating complex arrangements, governance & compliance, resourcing &

financing, mergers & acquisitions, management/team/board assessment, mentoring and strategic and tactical planning and implementation.

I received a Bachelor's of Business Administration from the University of Texas and a Masters of Management Science from the Alfred P. Sloan School at MIT. In 1996 I was awarded a Doctor of Philosophy by the Department of Government and International Studies, Strathclyde University, Glasgow Scotland with a focus in political and social theory and comparative cultural analysis. Subsequently I taught advanced political and social theory as an Honorary Senior Research Fellow at the Department of Government, University of Birmingham in England.

About This Series

As I look back over my experiences, the ones that I value above all are the times when I was able to help others. My fondest memories are of those times when a CEO faced a challenge that was truly daunting and was, with my help, able to overcome that challenge and grow in capability and understanding far beyond what they thought they were capable of. In a real sense, these books are written for those leaders who find themselves in similar situations - facing challenges that they are not sure they can overcome. The message that I very much want to communicate is 'Yes, you can overcome. Yes you can grow in mastery, understanding and knowledge. You can become so much more than you are."

This first volume is written as a series of 'thinking pieces'. Although there is an overall plan for the book, each chapter is designed to bring an issue into high relief and to help the reader get their mind around both the challenge and the way forward. I expect that you will find some of the chapters somewhat obscure at first but I urge you to persevere. No complex issue is mastered by a simple reading of a chapter or two. It takes thinking - reflection - living with new ideas - before some yield and real growth is possible.

We have all had the experience. Sometimes it takes weeks, months or even years to digest important lessons. Recently I finally came to understand something that a mentor had tried to teach me more than a decade ago.

For what it is worth, I suggest that you resist the temptation to 'blow through the book'. At the core of each chapter is a suggestion that will lead you to reconsider how you have been approaching a particular challenge and how you might change your behavior, approach and understanding so as to master it. Impatience carries a terrible cost when it comes to such changes in behaviors. The time you spend thinking about each chapter will prove much more valuable than the brief time you spend reading it.

The intent of this series is to give you the beginnings of insights - set you on the path that will result in your growth and mastery - open up the potential that has always resided within you. Be true to that project and our partnership will yield benefits far beyond your expectations.

About this Volume

One early autumn weekend three friends decided to head to the local fishing hole for a couple days of relaxation. Two of them were regulars at the lake. Their friend had heard so many stories about the fish, the camping and the comradery that, when he heard about the trip, he signed on immediately.

Now, as it happened, there was something peculiar about these three friends that bears mentioning. You see, each was a senior member of the clergy of their particular religion. One was a Rabbi of great reputation who had spent a lifetime studying the Torah. The second was world renowned scholar of the Koran. Now these two where neighbors who had retired to the shores of the lake to enjoy each other's company and the bounty that the lake provided.

The third member of the gathering was a bit different. For one, he was considerably younger. Yet to even begin thinking about retirement, he spent his time teaching at a major Catholic university. Now both a priest and widely respected scholar, he was in the prime of his career.

The three had met over the years at a number of ecumenical gatherings designed to increase understanding and communication among their great religions and, as friendships developed, spent private as well as public time together.

Now, back to the story. The three friends arrived at the lake early Saturday morning and decided to get in some fishing before even setting up camp. Hurriedly, they got the canoe in the water and headed out. After about an hour, the Rabbi said, "I'm thirsty and left my water bottle in the car. I'll be right back". At that, he stood up, stepped out of the canoe and walked across the surface of the water to the shore. Once there, he got the water bottle and walked back to the canoe and resumed his seat.

The event had two different impacts on the remaining occupants of the canoe. Our Koran scholar smiled and shook his head. But the priest went silent and pondered what he has just seen.

The Rabbi received a wink about half an hour later when his fellow retiree said, "You know, I've got just the lure to get these fish biting." He then proceeded to stand up, step out of the canoe and walk to the shore. Upon his return, he resumed his sera as if nothing particularly remarkable had happened, tied on the lure and proceeded to cast it out.

The third friend was lost in thought and pondering the amazing spectacles that he had just witnessed. He quickly came to the conclusion that it was a test of faith. He knew in his heart that his faith was just as strong as his friends so he spent some time in prayer and finally felt he was ready. "I forgot my hat. I think I'll go get it." He then stood up and stepped out of the canoe. Down he went into the water. His friends did the best they could to suppress the urge to guffaw but made little progress when faced with the vision of their friend trying desperately to climb out the water. Finally the Rabbi winked back at his friend and said, "I suppose we should tell him where the rocks are before he drowns!"

As the subtitle of this book indicates, this particular volume is written as a series of 'thinking pieces' that are to serve as points of meditation on important matters. Think of them as rocks leading to the shore. I'll leave you to figure out what and where the shore is, the canoe signifies and what's the reason for the journey. Those are yours to decide. All I intend to do is provide a general map of where the stones are. I wish you well on that journey and hope that my map is of some use to you.

About Me

I provide mentoring to those who have both the courage and determination to make a truly transformational journey. My approach is heavily influenced by core principles of Zen Buddhism. I don't offer quick fixes or follow the latest fads. If you are willing to make the long journey – if it's time for you to come to know the person you really are and can become – if you intend to finally find the path you should be following – if you want to start living life you were truly meant to live – then perhaps we should talk. Send me an e-mail and we'll arrange a time to chat.

Dr. Earl R. Smith II
Georgetown, Washington DC
June 2014
DrSmith@Dr-Smith.com

Table of Contents

~~~~~~

Yes You Can

It is a typical conversation which generally comes more than once during the initial months of most of my mentoring engagements. The client – generally younger and less experienced than I am – will insist that something is beyond their capability. I will insist that it isn't. And so I urge them to attempt – and they demure.

- You can do this!
- No I can't!
- It isn't rocket science – just think it through and do it
- But what if I screw it up?
- Then we will have proven that, contrary to your self-image, you are human after all (grin)

Sometimes this conversation comes when they are preparing for a major meeting – sometimes it precedes a conversation with a subordinate who needs to accept a new vision of his role. Each time it is a source of apprehension – mostly because:

There is something important at stake

It may be something which they have never done before or done badly in the past

I know that they are going to attempt it – an aware audience can be daunting – but also motivating

Trying new things – attempting new approaches to complex challenges – can be daunting. Everybody has their comfort zone and, by definition, these forays involve movement outside of that zone. But it is far easier and far more likely to end up positively if you have an experienced coach working with you. Here are a few of the steps which I help my clients work through:

- **Define the challenge**: Let's get a really good understanding of what needs to be done

- **Evolve the metrics**: How are we going to measure results and determine success or failure – let's get it clear

- **Define success**: What will a successful effort mean – what will be the results most desired?

- **Strategic into tactical**: Now let's work out a plan to achieve that success – starting from today and planning every step which needs to be made. This approach works particularly well when the challenge is a discrete event such as a meeting or discussion with a subordinate

- **Define the metrics for success at each step**: We generally end up with something that looks a lot like a Gantt chart – with starting and ending points for each step along the way and milestones for each major accomplishment

- **Design the monitoring process**: This is one which most of my clients tend to overlook at first. How are you going to track your progress and who are you going to review that progress with – and how often? The idea here is to be accountable to someone for your progress

- **Sharing the plan**: Who are you going to share the plan with and what are their roles going to be in the process? It is particularly important to identify critical contributions and the steps necessary to guarantee them

- **Resourcing the process**: What resources – funding, meetings, materials, etc. are you going to need? What arrangements are needed to make them available?

- **Contextualizing the challenge**: How does this particular challenge fit into the broader picture? Is this one a variation on others which you have successfully met in the past?

- **The ongoing postmortem**: The process of review continues throughout the effort – up to, through and after the challenge. The key lesson is flexibility and adaptability – you do, then review, then modify plans, then move forward. The review session generally produce a great deal of insight – personal epiphanies.

As the saying goes 'fortune favors the prepared mind'. By helping my clients work through new challenges, I increase the probability that they will have a successful experience – and successful experiences are the very foundation of a building confidence which leads to mastery of what, at first, appeared, beyond them.

~~~~~~~~~~

Grant me the wisdom ..."

That's how the old saying starts off. The rest makes a distinction between 'what I can't and can change'. Wisdom, it is posited, knows the difference – accepting what can't be changed and changing what can. Clear enough as it is but there is a wrinkle – an oversight – that most people routinely make – one that flies in the face of such 'wisdom'. They focus almost exclusively on what can't be changed

The behavior is ubiquitous among humans. It arises because we possess memory and can reflect on the past. It is said that a 'human is the only animal that knows it is going to die'. That may be so, but its Achilles heel is that it 'knows' it has a past and suffers all sorts of maladies because of its selective memories of it.

Mentoring Against the Past: In every mentoring session there are three entities in the room – my client, myself and the clients 'manufactured version of their own history'. The latter words have been chosen very carefully. It is not the client's history that is in the room. Nothing remains in the present except memories of it. But those memories are potent and often overmastering.

The challenge is to move past – or around – those memories. They are generally positioned between the client and me – held out as a 'true representation' of who that person is. But, of course, a mask is not a person and memories are not the past – only a present manifestation of a suspicion of having had one. But, as I said, they are potent – and a force to be reckoned with when trying to change behaviors, improve results or chart a new course.

The Past is Dead, The Future is Not Yet Here – There is Only Now: The past and future are very seductive inducements against living in the present. Most humans have a great deal of difficulty freeing themselves from the bondage. This freedom is an essential step towards claiming the present and forging a future which is not a minor variation of the past.

A person's past – or more exactly, their residual memories of their past – is a persistent and difficult adversary standing foursquare against change. Its power comes from the fact that, no matter how many times you look at it, nothing but your memories of it can be changed. I refer to this as 'moving the flatware around on the table.' You can readjust the memories – soften some and sharpen others – reorder them and highlight or dim as you please but you are still working on a dead project. Solutions to present challenges do not come from such activities. The activity in the present is just rearranging and reinterpreting the past – renovating an allusion.

Change Begins With 'Now': I work with clients to abandon the search for 'reasons why' and begin to focus on 'ways how'. My mantra is that reasons are only rationalized justifications that will get you nowhere – knowing why you behave in certain self-limiting or self-destructive ways is only an intellectual curiosity. Figuring out 'how' you are going to change the behavior – what your first step is going to be along that journey – now that is the real way out. You change by moving away from who you are towards who you are becoming.

This is not an easy journey – and not one to be attempted alone. My own was made with the help of mentors and mentors who took the time and made the effort to show me the way. My work with clients is, at least in part, a homage to the contributions they made to my life. Over the years, I have come to know the satisfaction they must have felt by helping me see a clearer way forward to a life which wasn't a minor variation of my past.

Don't make tomorrow's journeys using yesterday's maps

~~~~~~~~~~

Decisions, Decisions

Many of my mentoring engagements are with CEO's who are dedicated to improving their abilities and growing into their ever changing and expanding roles. One of the areas which we tend to focus on is the decision-making process. Interestingly, it is actually the pre-decision part which gives most of them problems. I regularly encounter clients who spend a great deal of time and energy dreading the meeting or situation in which they will have to make and implement an important decision. Then there are clients who, under the pressure to make such a decision, race right to making it in order to relieve the tension. Both end up with unanticipated first and second order effects from their actions.

After years of work with senior executives, I came to realize that these types of situations – and the two coping behaviors which are frequently adopted – are evidence of an aversion to the unknown. It is that apprehension which drives what turns out to often be counter-intuitive and counter-productive behaviors. Maybe it is the first time a CEO is faced with the challenge of re-negotiating an agreement with a senior team member – or perhaps it might be the need to restructure the relationship with the company's board. In each case, the executive is entering uncharted territory. In every case, it is the apprehension that causes the hesitancy and most of the collateral damage.

The clearest way I might explain what I mean is by using the example of getting into a pool. Let's say you go to a pool – you stand back and look at the water – worry that it might be cold – and hesitate to get in. There are lots of people already in the water – so the temperature is clearly OK – and will be after you get in – but that doesn't eliminate your apprehension. You hesitate – maybe dip a toe in – and then wade a bit at a time into the shallow end until – after an agonizing few minutes you are finally in up to your neck. The apprehensions which you allow to dominate your actions generate your behavior. But all of these things are manufactured complexities – the water is the temperature that it is and probably well within the 'acceptable' range. You know from past experience that, once you get in, the water will be fine. But you allow a manufactured unknown – a manufactured apprehension – to control your actions. Because you keep the water at a distance you cannot experience its 'reality' – and so it remains an unknown.

But let's look at the situation from another point of view. There are, of course, knowns – things that you can and need to be sure of before you get into the pool – like can you swim, is the water too deep, is the area that you might dive into too shallow or too crowded? But these are easily quantifiable. You do know if you can swim or not. You can see the pool and the people in it. You can choose the end of the pool you get into. And, like any rational decision, you can consider and evaluate all these based on personal experience and visual evidence. But what is the temperature of the water? That is the great unknown and the very thing that causes you to hesitate. But come on – you've been in pools before – you know that, once you get in, the water will be fine. Still you hesitate. And the only way to test the water – the only way the question can be answered – is to get in the pool.

The moral of this story is 'the only pain you can avoid is the pain you cause yourself by avoiding'. The water will be what it is – and the experience of diving in will also be what it is –

but the experience of the apprehension – of standing on the sidelines and dreading – that is a pain of your own manufacture – and it is completely unreal – virtual.

There is one more aspect of this process that I find fascinating. People who regularly cause themselves discomfort by avoiding decisions which take them into unknown regions also tend to have a distorted vision of the reality which they are facing. By that I mean that they tend to reduce situations to much simpler formulations and to clutter it with all sorts of completely incidental trappings. This is a very strange phenomenon – one which baffled me at first. Discussions about their behavior generally ran through all sorts of emotional and quasi-logical terrain – the 'human' aspects of which were often very convoluted – but seldom related directly to the situation and challenge before them. But their analysis of the decision tended to be overly simplified – reduced to a formulation which was clearly at odds with even a casual review.

Both of these behaviors combined to self-sabotage the person's ability to generate a positive outcome. It wasn't just the loss of time and opportunity – it was the corrosive effect of allowing this hesitancy to dominate the process – that was the real cost.

I have developed an approach to this type of situation which works remarkably well – and regularly use it in my mentoring engagements. The keys are to quantify the unknowns, increase an awareness of the process and the limitations that certain behaviors produce, develop the tools for a more realistic situation assessment and then lead the client through several of these decisions – until the new approach becomes a reflex. Now, after years of refinement, the approach works every time. It is a real joy to see clients now successfully dealing with challenges that used to turn them into the proverbial 'deer in the headlights' or the 'bull in the china shop'.

How Do You Decide?

Most people don't spend much time thinking about how they decide something – they are too busy deciding. But knowing how and why you decide can make the difference between finding your true path and wandering along a series of blind alleys.

~~~~~~~~~~~~~~~~~~~~~

Many of my life mentoring engagements initially focus on the question of how we decide to do what we do – be with the people we are with – live where we live – and so on. Sure, most of my clients have not put a lot of thought into the question – and that makes it interesting to them. However, the real benefit from asking it comes because it touches on issues that are central to the human experience. How you decide not only determines how you will live your life – it also determines what kind of a person you have and will continue to become.

The assessment process that I use for life mentoring is a bit different from the ones I use in either executive or leadership mentoring. The life mentoring approach is much more personal – centered on the individual and their approach to living. Three 'ways of deciding' tend to show up in the results of any assessment.

Accidental Decisions: "I don't know how it happened, it just did." If you kept track of the number of decisions you make during an ordinary day, the large number would surprise you. We make decisions all the time – some incidental and rather unimportant – others monumental in their implications. The former kind comes in herds – lots of them – and we make them without thinking much about either the implications or the facts surrounding them. We just decide – and, in deciding, we roll the dice. These random decisions tend to lead us towards other unanticipated – accidental – decisions. We make them often in the same way that we made the decisions that lead us to them – casually and without a lot of thought. These casually made decisions can bring us to big decisions unawares of their significance and, before we know, we have chosen.

Inertia Decides: "I'm happy with the way my life is." Inertia comes in lots of forms. Technically, inertia does not mean staying on one place but staying in one state. An ocean liner under steam has inertia – it moves in the same direction and is difficult to stop or turn. A rock has inertia – it sits on the ground and is heavy to lift. The antidote to inertia is change and it is the aversion to change that preserves it. Some people see inertia as 'familiar' or 'comfortable'. For them, life continuing pretty much as it has been makes a lot of sense. Habits are the most noticeable evidence of this tendency towards inertia. Habits tend to keep us within narrow channels. We make decisions based on them and, in the end, nothing much changes. The problem is that life is change and change means breaking inertia and moving on to another way of living.

Reacting Decides: "I just couldn't stand being in the same room with him." Reactions can be aversions or attractions – and many things in between. We sometimes react out of our current state of mind – loneliness, hunger, greed, melancholy and more – and that reactivity more than the facts of the decision we face, makes the decision for us. One of my life-mentoring clients had an aversion to large, open rooms that were noisy and crowded. His adversaries actually figured this out and maneuvered him into those conditions whenever possible. In his 'reactive state' he was capable of making al sorts of mistakes – and sometime did. The point is that reactive states can drive your decision process and cause you to make choices that are not in your best interest.

So, how do you break these cycles? How do you take control of your decision process and avoid the potholes of accidents, inertia and reaction?

The process begins with thinking. A quote from Inherit the

Wind may help. It starts with a question that goes to the heart of the matter.

Why do you deny the one thing that sets us above the other animals? What other merit have we? The elephant is larger, the horse stronger and swifter, the butterfly more beautiful, the mosquito more prolific, even the sponge is more durable.

The question that I put to my life-mentoring clients is 'why do you deny yourself the benefits of this singular merit'? Well, why do you?

The truth is that you do not have to be a victim – you do not have to suffer the *slings and arrows of outrageous fortune.* You do not have to be an alien in your own world. Do not look at the past and ask why. Look to the future and ask why not.

~~~~~~~~~~

Running On Empty

I recently took on a client who came to me through a good friend. She – his friend – was concerned for him and wanted me to help him if I could. Years ago, they had founded a company together and built it up to the point that another, larger company had decided that they just had to have it. The cash out was very good and both of them took off with their respective families for an extended and well-earned vacation.

When they finally got back together some six months after the sale, my friend was shocked at what she found. Her former partner was a mere shell of himself. The energy and enthusiasm that were his hallmark was gone. The glint in his eye and eagerness for meeting and besting the competition was gone as well. What made their meeting so poignant was she came back ready for battle and had anticipated that he would as well.

After an initial meeting I agreed to work with Daniel. To be honest, his case intrigued me. Although I didn't have the prior experience with him that my friend had, I suspected early on that there was something going on that was very important. It took a while to sort it out.

Quo Vadis Domini? Instead of approaching the question of his lack of enthusiasm frontally, I decided to take a more oblique approach. Sometimes the walls that are built around the face of a challenge are far more formidable than those guarding the other approaches. This turned out to be the case with Daniel.

We started out by identifying interests that we shared and exploring them together. Cigars and good whiskey were two that we quickly identified. Very bad science fiction movies quickly were added to the list – the kind where you can see the zippers on the monster's costume. Later on we discovered a common interest in Nietzsche and post-modernist philosophy. All of these shared interests allowed us to develop a solid friendship and a relationship of trust.

~~~~~~

Sometimes you have to start out left in order to go right

~~~~~~

When we finally turned to the core questions, the conversation was no longer between a stranger acting as coach and a person who used to be sure but was no longer. There is a reason that this was so important. The questions that he was asking himself were so close to his sense of identity that only in such an environment could they be discusses seriously.

Charting Your Own Course: Daniel had a confession to make. He had lived with the feeling that his prior life was made up by someone else and handed to him like a movie script. *"I'm feeling like I've been an actor mumbling the lines written for me by someone else"*, he observed. When we drilled down into that feeling, it became clear that he felt that way about his former partner as well as his parents and friends. *"I feel like I am running on empty. Everything that I have done – all the success that I've achieved – seem to belong to someone else. I need to find my own life and live it authentically."*

I've encountered similar feelings by some of my clients. Sometimes it comes early on and, with others, it comes late in life. But the dynamics are always the same. The energy that drove them on to do things because they could do them seems to have brought them to a place where that energy has dissipated – leaving them feeling hollow and directionless. Now they face the challenge of doing things because they really want to do them. And the question comes – what do I really want to do.

Sitting and Thinking is Quitting and Stinking: Once we had

the issues out in the open, my challenge to Daniel was to take the first step. *"In what direction,"* he asked? *"I don't care,"* I replied. Clearly frustrated, he shouted back *"how do I know which direction is the right one?"*

"There is no right direction. There is only movement from where you are towards somewhere else. Take the first step. Make a change. Do something different."

Things got warm between us over the next few sessions. Daniel was frustrated because he couldn't decide what he wanted to do or figure out how to make the first step towards doing it. It took me a long time to get him to understand that sitting where he was would not help him answer the question. *"You can't experience the incredible range of cuisines that bless the world by reading cookbooks,"* I said. *"Thinking about doing is not doing. It is not doing. Get off your ass and move."*

Enter the Nomad: During one session, I gave Daniel a map of the downtown area and a set of darts. We put the map on the wall and I said, *"go ahead – throw the darts".* He threw five of them. *"OK,"* I said, *"now, near as you can, identify the buildings under the points of those darts and systematically go through them – floor by floor and office by office. Come back after each one and tell me what you found. Some will take you days – maybe as much as a week, but keep at it."*

"Do you mean that I should give you a listing of the tenants in each building," he asked incredulously? *"No,"* I replied. *"I want you to go find out who those people are, what they do and why they do it."*

Well, the first building was a real challenge until he ran into a real character that showed him the way. This was a fellow who had passed along the same path as Daniel and had remade his life. Daniel became so fascinated with this character that he ended up buying him lunch. (They are now very good friends.)

In his wanderings my nomad found several others who touched him in similar ways – perfect strangers making perfect contributions to his life. He also learned that there are more ways to live a life than he had thought – more ways to make a living – more ways to discover and follow his passion. We've not closed the book on the mentoring work but we have filled the tank. Daniel is no longer running on empty.

~~~~~~~~~~

A Cost of Anti-Humanism

Much is made these days of the extended reach that all of us have gained because of the development of 'communications tools' like the internet, e-mail, social marketing sites and professional and social networking organizations. But there are costs that don't seem to find their way into discussions about this brave new world of interconnectivity.

It seems to me that several important components of human relationships have taken a beating over the last several decades and that the denigration of their importance and value is directly related to the anti-humanist nature of the new technologies and new vision of how humans develop and maintain healthy relationships.

Anti-Humanism

For my purposes here I am using the term anti-humanism to mean an individual's preference for technology-mediated relationships which insulate them from direct contact with other individuals. Elsewhere I have written about the tendencies which result in this preference but here I want to focus on some of the collateral damage that it causes to the very fabric of any culture and to the people who inhabit it.

Freedom to be an Avatar

Probably the most notable [advantage] of technology-mediated relationships is the incredible flexibility that it allows when it comes to self-definition. This advantage comes from the ease with which a person can 'make up' a personality or history and promulgate it with relative impunity.

At the core of this [freedom] is the proposition that who you represent yourself to be should have more to do with who you should be or need to be than who you are or ought to be or are. The ease of this creation induces a tendency towards larceny – sometime on a truly epic scale.

This behavior is 'empowered' by the very nature of internet-based technologies and the fact that most of the people participating are simply stretched too thin to be bothered with the efforts of verification let alone disclosure. To say it another way, the relationships simply do not have sufficient substance or importance to make it worth the effort to verify the truth or lies. The internet, in all its incarnations, prefers the avatar to the person – the digital representation to the messy details that each human represents. And those who use it are forced into this value proposition or marginalized as static.

Pretty much since the 60s Americans in particular have been worshiping in this anti-humanist temple. At the same time that traditional culture was dissolving – families were breaking up and dispersing – and a vocal generation was insisting that they had a new vision for society – technology was advancing in ways which would allow the refinement of this new anti-humanist vision of human relationships.

You see, the real challenge of direct human contact and deep personal relationships is to a person's vision of self-worth. In the anti-humanist vision of reality, the difficulties of building and maintaining such relationships came to be seen as unnecessary overhead – there is an easier, far less painful and exposing way.

Veracity Where Art Thou?

When Avatars define existence one of the first casualties is the idea of veracity. If you can make up whom it is that you present yourself to be then why not take a bit of literary license and embellish?

The transition here is from the traditional idea that every individual is the author of their own life to the idea that every individual is the author of the virtual representation of their virtual life. Once that leap has been made the entire idea of non-virtual veracity becomes an inconvenience.

Think about it this way – what are you really to an avatar with whom you have [connected]? Mostly you represent an occasional e-mail – a stream of ones and zeros – a co-conspirator in the game of mutually agreed upon self-deception and self-denial – a consenting player in the great anti-humanist game – a safe haven from the reality that refuses to cooperate or play the game by the rules.

Within the confines of the virtual, relationships become disposable and the threshold for their abandonment becomes very low indeed. Because there are so many opportunities for new, fresh avatar-to-avatar [connections], why fuss over one that has become a bother. A click and it is gone.

One of the surest triggers for that 'click' is the request for veracity – an effort to see behind the mask that is the avatar. The entire anti-humanist project is to provide protection from the prying eyes of others – a mask that hides the naked truth. And to understand why that is such an offensive request, we need to take a look at the relative values of the real and virtual.

Which is Truer?

Anti-humanist existence – if it is to be tolerable at all – depends on the revision of values – in fact, the inversion of values. What is 'real' cannot be allowed to be true until the definition of what is [real] has been transformed to mean what is defined as [real] in virtual terms. Once this jump has been made, the idea of truth becomes benign and completely supportive of the anti-humanist project – the accommodation had been made.

Here is an example. I occasionally have had people recommended others to me. When I ask "how well do you know them" I get "I met them online – they seem to be a great person." Further inquire only brings a repeat of the original description. I realize that their support of this person's avatar is based on an acceptance of the truth of that avatar and a calculated ignorance of the person who exists behind it.

But why ratify the virtual? That question bothered me for quite some time until I realized that it wasn't ratification but self-ratification that was in play. By representing the avatar of the other as real they were doing the same for their avatar(s) – it was a re-statement of the rules of the game and an announcement that they have accepted those rules and would comply completely. In other words it was a declaration of the abandonment of the true self for the virtual one.

Provisional Morality

The current generations are likely to go down in history as some of the most morally corrupt in history. That is not because they are essentially evil – but because the entire idea of morality is now considered mostly tangential to human relationships. Whole industries have evolved based on the marketing of lies – a now socially acceptable form of parasitic behavior. No longer is the onus on the provider to be ethical – honest and considerate – but on the buyer to avoid being taken in. But in a virtual world all there is is being taken in and all there are are buyers!

Once morality has been relegated to 'provisional' status, the field opens up to all sorts of behaviors which can be legitimized merely by the contention that they are ethical. Once the virtual demonstration of ethical behavior becomes the currency of determining morality, the entire world becomes a silly putty mass that can be formed and reformed at will.

Identity Theft

It is notable that the crime of identity theft is thriving in a virtual world that began with the anti-humanist intention to abandon identity in favor of virtual identity. Identity theft is really the theft of that virtual identity – the hijacking of the avatar. And the crime is only possible if the virtual has become more real than the actual.

But identity theft is not limited to subversion of entire avatars – it also involves the denigration of concepts and ideals which have historically been important to a stable definition of the human self. For instance the idea of intimacy becomes transformed when it is intimacy with avatars. One of the great assumptions of the anti-humanist project is that humans can do without all sorts of things that they thought they really needed. Technology modifies this assumption – humans can exist on virtual representation of those things which they thought they really needed. I strongly suspect that this assumption is tragically wrong.

Ephemeral Accountability

All that is virtual is ephemeral – it has no enduring substance and, therefore, it bears no responsibility for its actions or their costs.

Although this statement might sound strange, it is as true as true can be. Think of it this way – would you blame a ventriloquist's dummy for a murder committed by the ventriloquist simply because that dummy was the weapon used to commit the crime? An avatar is a virtual representation – made and presented without any necessary reference its veracity – is, in fact, a ventriloquist's dummy – only it is made of bits rather than wood.

The mask hides the true criminal and the crimes begin with the deception of the creation of the mask. But, if the only relationship is with the avatar, what or who do you hold accountable? The anonymity of the person behind the avatar – carefully protected by law and technology – is insulated from such accountability – as are those who provide the mechanisms to constructing and promulgating the masks.

Humans now find themselves unaccountable for acting humanly – and all who they relate to are strangers – and virtual strangers at that. No one is a person – only bits of data. There are no individuals – only data to be exploited. The very nature of relationships becomes both predatory and calculatingly deceitful.

Caveat Emptor All Around

The very nature of this new form of [human relationships] is that in a fundamental sense we are all, to the extent that we consent to participate in the anti-humanist project, buyers – buyers of the entire idea that the virtual is the new reality and that there is enough substance and sustenance in the virtual to satisfy human needs to be a social animal. But I suspect that there is danger in this assumption and that a [truth] unproven is no better than a [validated] lie.

~~~~~~~~~~

A Non-Cumulative Life

One of the most common challenges that my mentoring clients face is coming to terms with lost opportunities and broken connections. Many times the focus of our early conversations is on the number of years or decades that have been lived and the relatively meager accumulation of experience, lasting contacts and reputation that has resulted. Again and again I have begun work with someone only to find that one of their deepest fears are that the cumulative results of their life amounts to far less than they had hoped it would.

There are two avenues that have to be investigated and experienced in any such mentoring engagement. Both relate to behaviors – mostly self-sabotaging – and to the self-image that a person has developed and carries through life. Both are very difficult to address – particularly if a person tries to do so on their own. A good life coach can help overcome these difficulties and achieve breakthroughs that are truly life changing.

The Habit That Prohibits

In traditional societies individuals typically grew up within a matrix of relationships that foster long-term relationships with people who knew them, their history, family and personality. This matrix of relationships develops over the years into a network of long-standing connections which 'matured' into facilitating and supportive ones. One of the major values of these relationships was that they were inherently cumulative. By that I mean that they were a consistent and extended part of a person's history and insinuated themselves into the vision of self that comes to define a person – not only within their life context but within their own self-image.

But the breakdown of traditional society has produced an environment which does not provide such support. In fact, it has done quite the opposite – it facilitates a particularly difficult type of self-sabotaging behavior. At base humans are still very social animals – by that I mean that they have deeply felt needs for these long term connections. In an important way such relationships are the keel and rudder of the boat which is the person's self. The keel – that long spine that runs the length of most boats – provides directionality – keeps the boat on track – heading in a direction. The rudder both keeps the boat on course and allows it to change direction.

To see what I mean, consider the role of mentor in a person's life. Good mentoring relationships are about keels and rudders. A young person may have ideas and expectations about the world that are unrealistic – they may be expending lots of energy attempting to drive their craft in a direction which is damaging to their own self interests. The pressures of unfamiliar waters and poorly defined destinations may cause them to behave erratically and against their own interests. A good mentor helps to calm those waters, define directions, refine goals and adjust expectations.

But mentoring relationships are neither casual nor ephemeral. Faux mentoring relationships – ones that are called mentoring relationships but really aren't – are poor substitutes for the real thing. I have worked with clients who have spent years moving from one 'mentor' for another only to find that nothing much has changed – nothing has accumulated – other than the name of their current 'mentor' and an extending list of past 'mentors'.

For me the issue regularly comes into sharp relief as a result of another habit that I have. I journal and keep my calendars from past years – then once a year I spend time going back through them. One thing stands out every time – the number of broken threads – broken connections – missed opportunities and stagnant or attenuated relationships always seems much greater than I would have hoped for.

I call this behavior the habit that prohibits. Whether it arises from anti-humanism, a fear of intimacy, addiction to being anonymous, lack of patience or understanding of how such relationships arise, the net result always seems to be the same. People look back over their lives and realize that there is not as much there as they would have wanted or hoped for.

There is good news – as there always is when there is life yet to live. Individuals who find that their life is non-cumulative can change the behaviors which have produced the result. What has gone before is not necessarily the definition of what will occur from now on. It is a difficult journey that requires dedication and persistence – particularly at first – but it can be made.

Breaking the habit that prohibits means narrowing your focus to a smaller group of carefully selected contacts – no more 'open networking' with one surge of new contacts after another – no more non-cumulative behavior. You see it is your own behavior which generates a series of disposable relationships and overturns any possibilities that you might construct a context for yourself which supports and empowers it. It that sense, successfully breaking the habit that prohibits takes the same kind of effort and support as breaking any habit – like smoking or drinking or over eating.

The Vision That Clouds

A second issue is that many people simply don't know much about their lives and the relationships that they have built. Socrates said "*a life unreflected on is not worth living*". I would turn that quote around – "*a life unreflected on is often under-appreciated*".

Most of my life mentoring engagements begins with a detailed assessment of the client's life, current situation and broader context. After many such engagements, I have discovered that most people can produce a fairly detailed description of the first two but have only a vague and unfocused grasp of the last. To put it another way, people seem to have a better grasp on the immediate context of their lives than the extended one.

Quite often we will focus early efforts on discovering whether the boat really does have a rudder and keel. People who feel like they are drifting or that their life is out of control tend to assume that neither exist – and sometimes that is actually the case. But more often than not we discover that they really do – that there are foundational beliefs, long-term relationships and a more extended context which supports them.

This discovery – or, more properly, its rediscovery – is often a major step forward in the engagement. No longer alone in the dark night, the client realizes that there are others – and other communities – which are supportive and empowering. At the core of the epiphany, there is the discovery – the realization – that their life is much more than they have been thinking it was. I remember one client who came to me believing to her core that she was alone in the world – that only echoes within the darkness were her companions. Over the course of three months she discovered and re-connected with a wide range of people and groups. She came to feel buoyed up – supported – by them. Her discovery was that her life was far more 'cumulative' that she was allowing herself to accept.

Working Both Sides Towards the Middle

These are two 'habits' which sabotage life. Both relate to behaviors – one which sabotages future potential and the other which diminishes the past. The secret is to bring both of them into the present – to come to term with their implications in the 'now'. Until that happens nothing much will change.

Breaking the addiction to the habit that prohibits means overcoming the habit of prohibiting – a habit that is embedded within your own vision of what is possible and desirable. That means revising the values which seems to make the habit more desirable than what it is prohibiting. Overcoming the 'vision that clouds' means discarding the casual retelling of your life story – the avatar which you have created – and replacing it with a more accurate version. This means insisting on knowing yourself and being true to the truth telling of it all.

I have helped many people along this journey. In almost every case the results were a closer and more human relationship between a person and their life. Lives which were non-cumulative suddenly become cumulative. But it is only possible when you work both sides towards the middle.

~~~~~~~~~~

The Benefits of Quiet Time

There is danger in living on a non-stop endorphin high. In the first place, the human body is simply not engineered for such an existence. But more importantly the human soul requires an alternative to the nonstop, heated rush that such a life entails.

In my mentoring practice I regularly encounter people living peripatetic lives. They are constantly on the run ... and constantly under (mostly self-imposed) pressures. Their days seem to run together into a 'work hard – play hard' formulation. Most of them seem to be running in place or as the old country song suggests "climbing a ladder that leads to a hole in the ground".

When you step back and look at such a person's life and times, it is hard to tell the difference between them and any other beast of burden. Humans as oxen-pulling-the-turning-plow unrelentingly through well-tilled sod. The ox, having made the domestication deal, lives and dies without serious contemplation of purpose or direction.

I don't want to seem to be denigrating hard work, passionate dedication or dogged determination. All of these have a place in a productive and focused life. It isn't a question of either/or ... but one of balance.

When I was working on Wall Street I noticed that some of the very senior people seemed to have lots more time to reflect than those lower down the food chain. Initially I chalked it up to the intensification of the predator-prey dynamic ... the lower you are in the organization, the more likely you would act as prey ... the higher, the more likely as predator. Prey is always at risk ... predators took their time and picked their spots!

But, over time, I came to have a different understanding. I encountered people still on the lower rungs ... climbing the ladder ... but with apparently more time for reflection than their contemporaries. And they seemed to be outperforming them in the 'climbing'. They were just as driven as the competition but their lives seemed to be balanced differently. I began to think about the benefits of cultivating the habit of walling off sheltered time for slow breathing and thinking the higher thoughts.

After leaving Wall Street I started a number of companies and recruited and managed a wide range of team members, employees and partners. As luck would have it, some of these people were dedicated to making sure that they had regular time to think about what they were doing in terms different than just thinking about what you are going to do next. I learned a great deal from them and, as Robert Frost wrote, it has 'made all the difference'.

Then, while wandering around the high desert in the four corners region, I encountered an old shaman who took the time to teach me about the 'long body' … that vision of a human's existence that sees life from start to present and beyond in one continuous thinking. I came to realize that the old man was teaching me something profound. What I took away from that unendingly hot day and long, starry night has stayed with me. Time is neither a ticking clock nor a beating heart … it is a span of days that begins and ends in oblivion. It is only what we do between the goalposts that matters at all.

One of the things that I noticed early on in my work as a coach was that the sessions tended very early on to take on an almost 'alternate universe' aspect. By this I mean that the person seemed to shift into another reality at the beginning of each session. I took to thinking that they dropped their heavy coat and shed the halter, bridle and blinkers as they stepped through my door.

These people clearly wanted to spend time reflecting on this or that aspect of their business or personal life. They wanted to move into the more rarified regions of philosophical reflection and abstract thinking. I realized that they were looking to meet a very human, strongly felt need that was not being satisfied elsewhere in their life. In fact, the process of deciding to engage with a coach seemed, at least in part, to be predicated on a prior decision to meditate on the larger issues of living.

Because of these thoughts, I understand better my role as a coach. The Native Americans refer to a 'spirit guide'. Over and over again I have had the experience of helping a person clear away the obstructions and re-start their lives on a different footing. And I can tell you this above all … this is something that you can't do on the run or run down. You need to find and go into that quiet time and let it come to you. I will also tell you that the experience of helping another human to do such a thing is one of the primary reasons that I continue to coach.

~~~~~~~~~~

Seeking the Upward Path

There is a lot of writing being done on something called the 'Upward Path' or the 'Path'.

The recent TV series Stargate SG1 popularized the idea that it was possible to 'ascend' by finding and keeping to this 'path'. Most of this – including the TV series – is popularized and remanufactured bits of Buddhism. The problem is that it is misleading in several ways – that people who accept that 'seeking the upward path as the road to enlightenment' are almost certainly going to be seriously disappointed and waste a lot of living in what could only be called a 'kamikaze raid on a vacant lot'.

The basic problem with this form of pseudo-Buddhism is that it falls into a trap that Buddha himself warned against – the trap of grasping. A fundamental principal of Buddhism is that our problems are self-created through a tendency to hold on to artificial realities – like synthetic versions of our self or visions of the world as we would like it to be. This holding on is called grasping. According to Buddhism, you can't begin to move towards enlightenment by seeking enlightenment. That, in itself, is a form of grasping – grasping the ideal of enlightenment.

Many students and most 'casual' dabblers in Buddhism have a great deal of trouble getting their minds around this simple idea. For some it seems to take away all the purpose of 'practicing Buddhism'. I have had some ask me "*Well, if I don't have a goal, why practice Buddhism?*"

The presumption here is that the individual needs to be in control of their life – needs to direct it towards something that is presumed to have value. In modern terms "If you don't know where you're going how will you know when you get there?" The problem with this formulation is that it exteriorizes a journey which is essentially inward – the entire premise underlying the perspective assumes that the process is an outward journey – from here to there.

But the real journey in Buddhism is from here to here – from this present moment to this present moment. The goal is to be truly here – present in this moment – authentically and completely – without reservation or misunderstanding about either what or who is.

In a truer sense, the journey is down and inward rather than outward and upward. But in an even truer sense, the journey of a thousand years and a thousand miles is simply from here to here – no movement – no direction – no upward sloping path – only enlightenment that comes when the mind is finally quieted – the ripples calmed – perversions, misinterpretations and misdirection cast away.

Enlightenment is not a place to go to – it is a way of being. Not a single step in any direction is required to achieve it. Wherever you are it is there with you waiting to be discovered. If you travel half-way around the world seeking it, it will still be right there with you.

~~~~~~~~~~

The Passion Quest – Finding Your Center

Finding your path starts with finding your center. The hard truth is that other people are of little help on that inward journey of discovery. You have to do the heavy lifting yourself before you can finally meet the person you really are.

~~~~~~~~~~~~~~~~~~~~

My life mentoring engagements are a breed apart from my other ones. I enjoy working with leaders to develop their skills and abilities. Executive mentoring is fulfilling because I can see the advancements and the increased confidence that results. However, life mentoring is something else altogether. Here we are working at the very root of what it means to be human and to find a fulfilling life path.

I generally start life mentoring engagements with a question or two. Here is a sample:

~~~~~~~~~~~~~~~~~~~~

Do you love your life so much that you would actually pay money to live it? Do you wonder that you are being paid for what you do?

~~~~~~~~~~~~~~~~~~~~

Most of the time the answer is no. so I follow up:

~~~~~~~~~~~~~~~~~~~~

What are you prepared to do about that? How much of a commitment are you prepared to make to be able to answer yes?

~~~~~~~~~~~~~~~~~~~~

With that, one of the most important conversations in any human's life begins. The objective is nothing less than a search for passion in life. A common response is, "*I do not really want to feel this way. As it is, I am just not passionate about anything right now. How do I find my passion?*"

My life-mentoring clients have ranged from very senior and successful executives to people just starting out in life. One client – a very successful CEO – was making more money than he ever expected to. However, he felt that something was still missing. On the surface, his life appeared to be full and fulfilling. He had a good marriage, a family and occupied his free time with volunteering and interesting hobbies. He was looking for his purpose – wanted to find his passion.

Another client was just starting out. He had recently graduated from college and had landed a job that appeared to fulfill his best chances for establishing a career. However, he was suffering from the same malady. He was not passionate about it and was about to conclude that he would have to sacrifice his search for passion to the practicalities of making a living.

The Challenge

Both of these clients – and so many more of my life-mentoring clients – had made a decision that almost certainly doomed them to a career of increasing frustration and remorse for what might have been. They had accepted what life had offered them – an offering that was rather random and accidental – when they should have developed the self-knowledge that would help them go out and find the path that would lead to their passions. This single misstep put them on a downward path and delayed the possibility of them finding the upward one.

A major mistake that most of my clients have made before they come to me is that they assume that the job or the relationship will contain the passions that they are looking for in life – those passions are 'out there'. The answers are not 'out there' – they are 'in here' and the journey to them is inward rather than outward.

This misstep ignores the real value of every human's life journey – that it is unique and unique because the individual taking it is unique. Passion does not exist in the world in which we live, it exists and grows within us. We find it there or we will never find it. You can find and ignite those passions within you. When you do, the external world has a miraculous and magnificent way of rearranging itself to suit the person you really are.

The Passion Search

All of us have the ability to transform ourselves. However, it is not as simple as a shift in our perspective. It takes commitment and extended effort. The first part of any search is an assessment of things as they are – but not with a focus on the negative – a search for those positive things that resonate for us. Sometimes the thread is small and takes following – but it is a start. At other times, it is the proverbial eight hundred pound gorilla that has been sitting in the middle of the room all the time – grinning back at us. The search begins in earnest when you make that inventory and the commitment to follow the threads – or gorillas – wherever they lead you. Here is a suggestion:

1. Take an inventory – use a small notebook – carry it with you at all times – think of it as your 'detective's notebook' – you are on the hunt!

2. Spend some time looking for those threads that connect with things that you may be passionate about – do not give up after an effort that leads to none – stay with it – they are out there – find them.

3. Whenever you find a thread, make notes about it and follow up with an effort to expand on the focus – Google, search, ask people, read about it, find groups of people who share your interests

4. Pay particular attention to things you are grateful for – people you like to be with

5. Don't just focus on things – pay attention to experiences that make you feel good -that you would like to have over and over again in your life

6. Now take action – do something every day follow the leads – and build on them – remember, it is important that you cumulate – build on these thin leads – find your way into the center. I like to review my notebook at the end of the day – before I turn in. That habit seems to give me something to dream about. I wake up with a determination to do something that would take me closer to my passions.

7. Every so often, go back and re-read your notebook – find things that you may have missed – remind yourself of things that you have found – remember, cumulate

8. Finally, this journey is much easier if you have help – someone to keep you focused and motivated – someone to suggest things that you might have missed. As a life coach, that is a big part of my contribution. Remember, this is the most important journey that you will make in your life. It touches on all other parts of your experience. A good guide will make a big difference.

What's At Stake

More and more people are seeking life mentors. They realize that life gives you one chance to go around and there is no do-over button like there is on a video game. Make the commitment and stay with it. Seek out help and learn to benefit from it. It is your life – live it well and follow your passions.

~~~~~~~~~~

Ten Minutes That Will Change Your Life

~~~~~~~~~~~~~~~~~~~

Taking time to reflect – consider – learn – is one way to make your life richer and more fulfilling. It isn't hard to do – you don't need some gadget or prop – you just do it. But most people don't do it – and they suffer lost fulfillment because of that – and remain completely ignorant of the loss.

~~~~~~~~~~~~~~~~~~~

Pretty catchy title, don't you think? Don't you 'instant gratification' types get too carried away. I am going to tell you about a ten minute exercise that will change your life. That's the good news. The bad news is that it is a daily exercise. You'll have to find ten minutes each and every day for the rest of your life and work hard to convert this exercise into an enduring habit. For some of you ten minutes a day will prove too high a price for the possibility of changing your life. For others, and I hope most, it will be a small price to pay for a huge step forward.

So, it's not like a vaccination. You don't get one shot and then you're good to go for the rest of your life. But the only time that will ever be true is the second just before you die – and who wants to wait that long to achieve enlightenment?

When I first arrived on Wall Street, I became fascinated with people who seemed to be much better organized and focused than the other people around them. I was attracted to these people because they made much better partners and much more reliable participants in teams that I put together. They seem to avoid the 'muddling through' that characterized the daily lives of most of the others.

Some years later, as my Buddha nature began to emerge; I sought out a particular monk and asked about the relationship between my life and what I understood about it. The teaching which ensued helped me to understand what I had observed on Wall Street. Over the years the gift I received from this particular monk has become a habit – a highly productive and useful one. I'd like to pass on that gift if you're willing to listen, consider and learn.

The unexamined life is not worth living, Socrates

Examine Your life: Old Socrates sure had that one right. To leave a day without giving a thought about how that day has been lived is to waste the time and effort of living that day. It is more tragic than having lived a decade without reflecting on how that decade was lived. It is much more tragic than living a year without reflecting on how that year was lived. It is only slightly less tragic than living a moment without reflecting on how that moment was lived. What is the point of going into tomorrow if you haven't learned the lessons of yesterday? The truth is that, if you don't learn, you end up going back into yesterday all over again!

A person is condemned to confront the same challenge over and over again until they master it. Then they get to go on to the next one. Those of you who have been paying attention will find this statement a judgment on those who have not learned Socrates' lesson. I was, of course, referring to those 'deer in the headlights' types that you meet all the time. Much like a TV soap opera, they can pass out of mind for years and, when they return, their continuing lives seem like just more of the same. Making the same mistakes over and over is a sign of inattention – a sign of being asleep.

The simply ridiculous thing about the insight which Socrates delivered to humanity those many centuries ago – an insight which lies at the very core of Buddhist teachings – is that, like most fundamental truths, this enlightenment is more a

49

matter of dedication to simple actions than to mind bending mental gymnastics over Byzantine logic and convoluted theories of existence. But for the well-educated amongst us, the latter is always easier than the former.

By three methods we may learn wisdom: first, by reflection, which is noblest; second, by imitation, which is easiest; and third by experience, which is the bitterest. Confucius

The view from above: I will admit that there is a trick to all of this. The trick is that you must cultivate the ability to view your day from the outside of yourself – or, more properly, from above. If you can't manage that 'out of body' perspective, the sessions are likely to descend into a mire of self-congratulatory self-ratification.

In the course of your review you should look at your day as one who is observing it as it takes place. This 'observer's' perspective is critical to making the process productive. Some people get it when I describe the view as being the proverbial fly on the wall. Others understand what I mean when I suggest that you review your day as if you were watching a movie of it. No matter how you achieve this perspective, it is important because without it true reflection is impossible.

To achieve true reflection is to avoid the necessity of attaining wisdom either by imitation or by experience. Confucius had it right when he suggested that it is far sweeter to learn by reflection than to suffer the bitter cost of learning the other ways.

They only babble who practice not reflection. Edward Young

Ritual and a retreat to a private space: Everybody has to pick their own time of day. For me, it is the hour just before getting ready to go to bed. But the choice of the time of day is not as important as how well that choice is made for the individual choosing. Reflection on 'the day just lived' is best done in a quiet place that is soothing and conducive to reflection. It is important that the time and place be available every day and without exception.

My own ritual begins with the making of a cup of tea. I don't think about the day while brewing the tea – I think about brewing the tea. The water coming to a boil, the smell of the tea in my hand, the flow of water into the cup, the aroma that rises and fills the room as the tea brews – all of these things take my attention – and focus my senses on the present. This focus on the present allows my mind to settle out of whatever has occupied it during the day and into the very familiar patterns of preparing a simple cup of tea.

Your ritual will be different but you must pick it with care. Every day at the same time you should wall off the rest of the world and retreat into this private and secluded glade to reflect.

Without deep reflection one knows from daily life that one exists for other people. **Albert Einstein**

Listing your day: Here is the idea in a nutshell. At the same time each day you spend ten minutes thinking about the day you have just lived through. See your day through the eyes of someone who has been observing you. List every event, large or small – significant or insignificant, that occurred during the course of your day.

So I take my tea to a favorite chair. I sit back, relax and let my mind relax as well. Then, over the next few minutes, I slowly and carefully relive the day. My mind revisits each event – meetings, phone calls, things read, things thought about and conversations all get their chance to be revisited. In each case I am an observer of myself engaged.

> *Follow effective action with quiet reflection. From the quiet reflection will come even more effective action.*
> **Peter Drucker**

Consider each action: Once my listing is complete I start at the beginning of the day and relive each event – but not as a person that lived through the day but as an observer of a scene in which I am an actor.

Begin at the start of each day. Think about each action – no matter how minor – and try to revive the experience of one who has lived through it. When it was only you and there was no other person involved, try to view the experience as an interaction between you and your self. I know that's going to sound a bit loony at first but follow me for a bit. Every time you try to develop a new habit or improve yourself in any way there are those parts of you which oppose the change. We've all had that experience. So in some ways all efforts at personal improvement results in an argument with yourself. Ignore this argument and proceed with confidence.

Here's an example that might relate to your morning. Let's suppose you have resolved to rise earlier and engage in a bit of morning exercise. But your list shows something other than complete success in this area. By highlighting the fact that you did not meet your own expectations you reduce the probability that you will simply ignore your own under-performance through an act of personal indifference.

When an action involves another person try to relive that experience as one of serving the scene of two interacting. It will be difficult it first but after a bit of experience you should begin reliving those interactions as intensely, and often more intensely, then they seemed at the moment you lived through them. But your understanding of each event should be different than it first because of this new perspective.

It is a most mortifying reflection for a man to consider what he has done, compared to what he might have done. Samuel Johnson

Positive or negative … understood or misunderstood … kindness or abusiveness: As you relive each action that was part of your day you should start to notice your own behavior and how it influenced the outcomes. At first you won't be very good at this but eventually reliving each experience will begin to generate new understandings of how you interact with your own goals as well as with other people.

Sometimes as a result of reflection I come to realize, all be it several hours later, that my role in a particular discussion was positively negative. I will see myself turning an opportunity into a tirade on some minutia. At the time it went unnoticed by me but now it stands out in high relief. The other person (the bringer of the opportunity) certainly did notice. I make a note to myself that I owe that person an apology as well as an attempt to reconnect on the opportunity.

On another occasion, I might realize that I had spent a great deal of energy and effort trying to give a particular individual guidance that would help them overcome a very negative habit. During the actual effort and in the heat of the moment I was very involved in trying to get them to see the light. Later that day, as I relive the experience, I come to realize that I have had a number of conversations with this person on the same subject and with the same results – they have no intention of changing their behavior – their attitude is simply 'well, this doesn't work – let's to more of it.' As a result of reflection I realize that this person's self-destructive behavior is their business and not mine. Any attempt to help this person amount to the proverbial 'kamikaze raid on a vacant lot'. So I let it go and resolve to leave those pretending to be asleep pretending to be asleep.

One point of guidance in all of this – the objective is 'understanding' rather than 'self-recrimination'. In order to achieve that you must learn to be kind to yourself. You must cut yourself some slack – after all, most of you are human! The small joke aside, this is a very important idea. Reflection which results in self-abuse is simply masochism parading as self-help. If any of this is going to result in positive change you must approach yourself as a fallible human being who needs, and deserves, your support attention and understanding. During these sessions you'll find yourself shaking your head in disbelief – try to add a gentle, bemused smile while you're doing that.

If we would only give, just once, the same amount of reflection to what we want to get out of life that we give to the question of what to do with a two weeks' vacation, we would be startled at our false standards and the aimless procession of our busy days. Dorothy Canfield Fisher

Planning the renovations: One of the great benefits of reflection is that it helps you sort out what you can do from what is properly left on someone else's plate. By living through your day a second time you have a chance to see yourself in a different light.

The second great benefit is that reflection can lay the groundwork for planning and monitoring change and personal growth. Once you have begun to understand your own behavior from this new perspective the process of managing improvements in your understanding, responses and performance becomes considerably easier.

You should notice that your focus narrows to the practical and to those things which can be accomplished with focused effort. Most people suffer failure in their attempts at personal improvement because their goals are entirely too strategic. Focusing on individual actions during the course of a specific day will result in understandings that can be acted on immediately and with intent to generate specific improvements.

So now go back to your list and begin to fill in the action items. Each action is relived and a lesson is derived from the experience. What could have been done better? What did I miss that I should have seen? How could I have behaved differently and achieved a better result? What was this person trying to tell me that I didn't hear? Your list of questions will grow as you get better at reflection.

Every time one of these or similar questions resonates you should stop and think about how you're going to approach similar situations differently in the future. Make a note next to that action to remind you of this new resolution. At the core of this action is a resolved to make tomorrow a better day than yesterday – to make your participation in tomorrow better than yours was in yesterday.

Without reflection, we go blindly on our way, creating more unintended consequences, and failing to achieve anything useful. **Margaret J. Wheatley**

Your turn: Ten minutes is going to seem like a very long time at first – but after a week or two it will seem like not nearly enough. The habit of ten minutes flows into a life path that guides you to an entirely new vision of yourself and the world that you live in – and you will awaken to a new path for your life.

Ten minutes a day can, and will, change your life if you have the resolve to let it do so. Ten minutes a day – a mere sixty one hours a year – can open opportunities, disclose secrets, expand horizons and make you a far better person than you ever thought you could become. The first ten minutes will come and pass today. Use it or lose it. Decide that your life and future is worth that small sliver of time or get ready to live yesterday over and over again.

~~~~~~~~~~~

Change Aversion – Coming to Terms

Change is the one unavoidable aspect of living. Time and our lot as humans see to that. A good way to see personal growth is as the process of responding positively to that change. We all know that the idea of change can be unsettling. Many people see it as stepping from the known to the unknown. However, the only way that you can see it this way is to ignore that change is an unavoidable part of your every day. You are changing all the time.

Therefore, the question is not whether or not you will change but how big are the steps you are ready to allow yourself to take. Your personal growth depends on this very decision. Some people restrict themselves by allowing only very small steps while others reach the same result by insisting on very large ones. The issue is one of finding the correct balance – your comfortable stride, so to speak – and to begin to lengthen it gradually.

Stress over change comes from two sources. The first is the process of change itself – you have to pay attention to what is becoming the new 'reality'. The second is the apprehension that you bring to the process when you contemplate changes at your upper level of tolerance. Your ability to come to terms with change and grow will depend on how comfortable you can become with the first apprehension and how much you can reduce the second.

It is a truism that there will be no growth without effort. Change and the challenges that it brings is the common denominator. Your approach to change and ability to achieve the correct balance will define your life as much as any other factor – and much more than most. Turning the reality of change into meaning in your life is the important process – the way forward. Sorrows and your grief are nothing compared to mastering this process – in fact, they are lessened as you master it. Misfortune is part of living but your contribution to your own misfortune will abate as you master it. Good or bad fortune will come your way. Change will constantly remind you that you are alive. In order to find the meaning in your life and transform it into something of value, you must embrace the process – embrace each breath – and see each breath just as each day as the change that lets you know you are still among the living.

Life is change – embrace it with gusto!!

~~~~~~~~~~

Orthodoxy or Optimism?

I was having drinks with a friend a couple of weeks back when the conversation took a strange turn. As a matter of background, I have known him for a couple of decades, considered him a valued friend and someone who thought before he spoke. We were discussing alternative energy and the likely way forward. What set me back was his insistence that there was no future other than through existing technologies.

The center of his argument was that, by using oil, nuclear and coal, the United States could meet its needs for the foreseeable future. He disparaged solar (a filthy production process), wind (overblown), geothermal (over-hyped) and fuel cells (something out of Star Trek). Although we might disagree on the judgments, the major difference between us was how we viewed the future – he as pretty much more of the same and I as a new world, remade by new technologies. My initial thought that he was simply afraid of the future and, because of a failure of will, found his courage broken by challenges he could not see a way past.

That judgment set until, while reading one of my old journals, I came across something that another friend had said. He is long dead but his words seemed to resonate as I read them. "When orthodoxy becomes a substitute for inspiration, that person is walking dead, taking up space and breathing air best left to others." I realized that my live friend was simply spouting the orthodoxy being offered by entrenched interests. In other words, he was a mindless water carrier for people who either didn't know or care who he was.

Needless to say this was unsettling. I remembered an older saying – "the greatest tragedy is what dies in a man before his body dies".

As I went down that path, thinking about friends and their words, yet another friend intruded. Some hours later I was reading another one of my journals – one from three years later. Here was another friend contributing to the conversation. She was one of the greatest writers that England had ever produced and once said to me "boy (I was younger then) when ideology becomes a substitute for courage, when ignorance becomes a badge of honor and knowledge is disparaged, bend over and kiss your ass goodbye – the human race has lost its way and very purpose for being."

It is easy in this information age to find people who meet her description. People, for instance, who disparage the great insights of Darwin while neither understanding those insights or where they have subsequently lead. Other Americans are world leaders in self-delusion. They know nothing about most of the world and could care less. They speak only one language and that very badly. Still others see complexity in black and white terms and see simple minded solutions to complicated challenges. Then there are those who really believe that they are 'reality shows'. But these have always been 'those people over there'. Somebody else's neighbors. Now I found that the disease had moved in next door.

When I was at the Sloan School, I was working one evening – and well into the night – on a project for the Carnegie Foundation. I was in the basement of the computer center – that's where they had to put it so that they could keep the beasts adequately cool. About two in the morning I was thrown off my terminal. I looked around to see that everybody else had been thrown off as well. None of us were able to get back on – so we all headed home. As I was getting ready for bed, I turned on the television and heard the first news about Apollo 13. As the hours then days dragged on, I was struck by the mantra of the engineers – "failure is not an option; we are going to get those guys safely back".

Some years later I was watching another NASA briefing – the one about how the Shuttle's heat tiles might have been damaged during launch. One senior official said – obviously unaware of the presence of a microphone -"why bother to look at the heat shield? If it is damaged, they are dead already". I remember being stunned by this statement. When did 'failure is not an option' transmute into 'they are dead already'?

The truth is that we are living through a time when the nature of the American character is on the line. To borrow a line from Thomas Paine, 'These are the times that try men's souls'. There are those who, through a failure of will or sacrifice of ideology for intellect, would seek refuge in the twentieth century. Others seem to still have the old spark that a Scottish friend once defined. "You Americans always want to live in tomorrow before it even arrives".

Maybe it's time for all of us to look in the mirror – when you do, who do you see looking back?

Don't make tomorrow's journeys using yesterday's maps

~~~~~~~~~~

Knowing What Matters

It was during one of the first mentoring sessions with a new client that the following exchange occurred:

Me: Life is much like that path of a bird through the sky. It leaves no trace. There is only the bird and flight.

Client: So you are saying that your life and mine are like that.

Me: Yes, in a very important way. Living in the present makes all questions about such things meaningless.

Client: But that sounds like such a dark view. I would like to think that my life will leave a trace; that people will know that I was here and who I was.

Me: That is leaving the living of your life and tending to an artificial reality. You convince yourself that such a thing is so important that you abandon the chance to live.

Client: But it seems like such a waste. The bird leaves no trace in its flight. That is such a hollow way to look at it.

Me: Maybe for you, but how about for the bird?

That question seemed to be one that he had never

considered.

Me: What do you think the bird is experiencing? Living in the moment, with its intention to go from one place to another and doing just that. Do you think it worries about whether its flight leaves a trace? In the joy of flight and with the feeling of its wings providing lift do you think that such things matter much to the bird? The lesson here is that the bird is much better at being a bird than you are at being a human. The bird lives the exact moment it is living while you worry about moments past.

Some hours later I was sitting in a park on a sunny afternoon. A mockingbird flew out of the trees and across the meadow. I watched the bird's flight and wondered at its immediate experience of living. Clearly nothing mattered but the process of flying. Its intention was to do exactly that. About half way across the meadow it dipped down and soared up. I took it as a sign of the joy it felt at being just there in just that time.

The mockingbird knew what mattered and spent no time wondering about what did not. Of all its flights that had left no paths through the sky, there was the wonder of being able to fly through this one at this time. The bird was alive to the moment it was living.

Then there was another thought. I remembered how another bird in another sky and time had first taught me that same lesson. We humans can go far astray chasing things that simply do not matter. In doing so, we give up the chance to live in the moment and the wonderful experience that comes with simply being fully alive and present in the moment.

My client may have had the first glimpse of that insight. That mockingbird reminded me that even such a lesson is a trap and a diversion. We give up the immediate experience of living for such silly things as posterity. We lose track of what really matters. The bird's experience is his own. I spent the walk back to the office reveling in mine; and did not worry about not leaving tracks.

~~~~~~~~~~

Thoughts on Excuses

One of my favorite sayings is 'to excuse yourself is to excuse yourself. I recently intervened with a management team that had really messed things up – and that saying kept running through my head. They were masters of the excuse. There was a reason why or why not for everything. However, none of these reasons involved anything approaching personal responsibility for outcomes. What astonished me was how natural all this excusing seemed to come to them. The team had truly created a culture of excuses where a culture of achievement was called for. Now, at the end of the investor funding, they had run out of relevance. Their excuses meant absolutely nothing to anyone.

I did a quick search for sayings about excuses and gathered quite a few. Here are a some of the better ones:

Excuses are tools of the incompetent, and those who specialize in them seldom go far.

Excuses are tools of the incompetent used to build monuments to nothing. For those who specialize in them shall never be good at anything else.

An excuse is worse than a lie, for an excuse is a lie, guarded. Alexander Pope

Bad excuses are worse than none. Thomas Fuller

Don't make excuses, make good. Elbert Hubbard

Every vice has its excuse ready. Publilius Syrus

He that is good for making excuses is seldom good for anything else. Benjamin Franklin

He who excuses himself, accuses himself. Gabriel Meurier

Hold yourself responsible for a higher standard than anybody else expects of you, never excuse yourself. Henry Ward Beecher

If you don't want to do something, one excuse is as good as

another. Yiddish Proverb

Nothing is impossible; there are ways that lead to everything, and if we had sufficient will we should always have sufficient means. It is often merely for an excuse that we say things are impossible. Francois De La Rochefoucauld

The best job goes to the person who can get it done without passing the buck or coming back with excuses. Napoleon Hill

Two wrongs don't make a right, but they make a good excuse. Thomas Szasz

We are all manufacturers. Making good, making trouble, or making excuses. H. V. Adolt

We have forty million reasons for failure, but not a single excuse. Rudyard Kipling

There aren't nearly enough crutches in the world for all the lame excuses. Marcus Stroup

Excuses are the nails used to build a house of failure. Don Wilder

Difficulty is the excuse history never accepts. Edward R. Murrow

It is better to offer no excuse than a bad one. George Washington

We are all manufacturers. Making good, making trouble, or making excuses. H. V. Adolt

The real man is one who always finds excuses for others, but never excuses himself. Henry Ward Beecher

People with integrity do what they say they are going to do. Others have excuses. Laura Schlessinger

For many people, an excuse is better than an achievement because an achievement, no matter how great, leaves you having to prove yourself again in the future; but an excuse

can last for life. Eric Hoffer

Several excuses are always less convincing than one. Aldous Huxley

The trick is not how much pain you feel but how much joy you feel. Any idiot can feel pain. Life is full of excuses to feel pain, excuses not to live; excuses, excuses, excuses. Erica Jong

It is easier to find an excuse than to find a reason. Doug Brown

I attribute my success to this: I never gave or took an excuse. Florence Nightingale

Don't make excuses, make good. Elbert Hubbard

There's a difference between interest and commitment. When you're interested in doing something, you do it only when circumstance permit. When you're committed to something, you accept no excuses, only results. Art Turock

Ninety-nine percent of the failures come from people who have the habit of making excuses. George Washington Carver

You can give in to the failure messages and be a bitter deadbeat of excuses. Or you can choose to be happy and positive and excited about life. A.L. Williams

Difficulty is the excuse history never accepts. Edward R. Murrow

An excuse is worse and more terrible than a lie; for an excuse is a lie guarded. Alexander Pope

Excuses are the nails used to build a house of failure. Don Wilder

Ninety-nine percent of the failures come from people who have the habit of making excuses. George Washington Carver

There aren't nearly enough crutches in the world for all the lame excuses. Marcus Stroup

People are always blaming their circumstances for what they are. I don't believe in circumstances. The people who get on in this world are the people who get up and look for the circumstances they want, and, if they can't find them, make them." George Bernard Shaw

Never ruin an apology with an excuse. Kimberly Johnson

Uncalled for excuses are practical confessions. Charles Simmons

"Don't look for excuses to lose. Look for excuses to win." Chi Chi Rodriguez

"Love will find a way. Indifference will find an excuse."

"Good taste is the excuse I've always given for leading such a bad life" Oscar Wilde

"Bad things are always going to happen in life. People will hurt you. But you can't use that as an excuse to fail or to hurt someone back. You'll only hurt yourself."

"Man gives every reason for his conduct save one, every excuse for his crimes save one, every plea for his safety save one; and that one is his cowardice" George Bernard Shaw

"There's no excuse to be bored. Sad, yes. Angry, yes. Depressed, yes. Crazy, yes. But there's no excuse for boredom, ever." Karolvig Viggo Mortensen

"Pessimism is an excuse for not trying and a guarantee to a personal failure." Bill Clinton

"We have more ability than will power, and it is often an excuse to ourselves that we imagine that things are impossible." François de la Rochefoucauld

"Smokers, male and female, inject and excuse idleness in their lives every time they light a cigarette." Sidonie Gabrielle

Colette

"Destiny: A tyrant's authority for crime and a fool's excuse for failure." Ambrose Bierce

"Every man ought to be inquisitive through every hour of his great adventure down to the day when he shall no longer cast a shadow in the sun. For if he dies without a question in his heart, what excuse is there for his continuance?" Frank Moore Colby

~~~~~~~~~~

The Importance of Acting on Good Ideas
In the Battle Against Inertia

"It is important to act on good ideas – I have not done that consistently."

I recently came across this in one of my old journals. I remember the feelings that were there when I wrote it. Acting on good ideas is part of personal growth – part of an effort at self-improvement. The mind comes up with these flashes of lightening but it is the body that drives them into action. So where does this leadership come from – what leadership style is needed to consistently turn good ideas into action? How do you become an adviser to yourself – and adviser who does more than urge action and regret the lack of it?

The trap is, of course, that the very pursuit of this question can sink into a cesspool of self-recrimination. And, in that action, yet another good idea will pass into the realm of 'good but not acted on'. The critical first step is leadership development – to bring forth the tendencies in your own reaction to good ideas that will increase the chances that they will be acted upon. And this step is more in the realm of spirituality than 'management'. The turn of mind that allows you to follow-up on good ideas begins with a re-envisioning of some very important parts of yourself. So let's talk about how you welcome – then deal with – 'good ideas'.

How often do you celebrate the arrival of a good idea? How often do you take leadership in the announcement of its presence? Think about it. Do you make a 'big thing' out of it or tend to hide the fact of its arrival – perhaps under the suspicion that you really don't get or deserve good ideas anyway. I'm not talking about blowing your own horn here – but blowing the 'idea's' horn.

How often do you feel grateful that you have been blessed with this good idea? It's one thing to recognize a good idea and yet another to realize that it came to you and not to somebody else. Do you think about that at all?

How often do you recognize a good idea for what it really is – a gift that you can give to others – a special something that will have value in their lives as well as in yours? The really marvelous thing about good ideas is that they don't disappear when you share them with other – most often they get even better and more valuable. In an important sense you become the Chairman of the Board of Directors of this good idea – help it grow and become something even more potent – more valuable.

Finally, how often do you recognize that it was you and not somebody else that had this good idea? This goes directly to your own self-image and you need to think about it carefully. Do you see yourself as somebody who generates good ideas or are good ideas just accidents that happen to happen to you?

Here's my suggestion – welcome each good idea and celebrate its arrival – feel grateful for having been chosen as the recipient of this marvelous gift – don't hide your good ideas but share them with other and contribute to the making of even better ideas – and remember always that it was you that came up with the idea and you that can come up with others.

~~~~~~~~~~

Giving Yourself Permission

This might seem like a strange idea at first – giving yourself permission – but, once you think about it some, you will realize that it really gets to the core of how you live – and decide to live – your life. Begin with this simple idea – you are the gatekeeper of your own possibilities – you determine what is possible for you.

Now, before you go on about the limitations of this mortal form, stop and remind yourself that what is important here is that you take leadership in – and responsibility for – your own personal growth. We are dealing with questions of spirituality not theology – and the core question is not whether, by the end of your life, you have learned how to live forever – it is whether during your life you've made the most of the advantages that you had.

In my life mentoring practice I encounter people who have never given themselves permission to sing or dance. If I ask them if they sing or dance they say no – but if I ask them why they don't sing or dance, the responses get less definite. Many times I introduce the idea of 'leadership style' or 'leadership development' – what kind of a leader are you being when it comes to deciding how to live your life? Initially the question brings a blank stare but, after some work, the real meaning comes clear. You see, life mentoring – indeed any mentoring or advisor role – is a matter of helping a person to accept that they are the author of their own life – they are the gatekeeper to their own possibilities.

One of the more delightful people that I have met in my journey through life is the American poet Robert Bly. He as written many great poems and a very valuable book titled *Iron John'*. One of his personal quirks is that he just can't seem to end a seminar, meeting or gathering without singing something. He always brings some ancient instrument and sometimes this leads to dancing as well. Robert has exuberance for life – just like all of us – but he has given himself permission to experience it and to show it to others.

Like Bly, we all have the exuberance for live bubbling inside of us. When you stop and think of it, it is a pretty amazing thing to be alive – and to be aware you are alive. But Robert has taken that great first step and given himself permission to experience that exuberance – and to let that exuberance show.

Hey, in the end what have you got to lose? When your ass is cold there will be plenty of time for withholding permissions. But for now warmth should be on the menu – the warmth of singing and dancing – the warmth of connecting, giving and receiving – and the of giving yourself permission to feel alive. Thinks about – but not too long – the grains of sand are running as we speak.

~~~~~~~~~~

Finding Your Path

Finding your path is a truly life-changing experience. Life is no longer uncertainty – your connection between living and your purpose in life goes with you every day. When you honor your possibilities – allow them to become realities – you become the person you always could be.

~~~~~~~~~~~~~~~~~~~~

All of us get lost occasionally. We find ourselves wandering or drifting – sometimes for years. Then one day we realize that the clock is ticking – the sand is running out of our own personal hourglass. Many of my clients come to me when they have reached such a time. They have lost their path.

My life-mentoring message is simple and direct. It does not have to be that way. Your life does not have to be the way it is. The journey back to the path begins with a new dream. To have a new dream you must begin to dream. Without dreams, the future is going to be a lot like the past. Most of my clients come to me because they have lost the tendency to dream.

The kind of dream that I am talking about is the one you have of yourself. How you relate to that self – how you honor the possibilities – is part of that dream. For some, the dream has become so mundane that they do not visit it anymore. For others, it is taken to be so offensive or depressing that they avoid all contact. It does not have to be that way.

The gateway to the dreaming is unreserved self-acceptance. Restarting the dream is often not an easy or comfortable process. The blocks to dreaming can be formidable. One of the most difficult to overcome is the suspicion that you do not deserve to have a dream. But, of course, you do. The dream is waiting for you – waiting to be dreamt.

Helping my clients begin the dream anew is the place where

most of my life mentoring begins. The need to accept their value as a human being and that that value is positive. They need to accept that they are deserving of the dream and all the things that it can bring them. They need to give themselves permission to reach for the possibilities that the dream shows them. It can be that way.

Too many people take their own value for granted. They overlook or devalue the great and good things in their life. They forget that life itself is a wondrous gift of in great value. It does not have to be that way.

Life mentoring is about helping another person rediscover and reconnect with his or her dreams. As I work with them – help them reconnect and overcome challenges – they begin to awake to the possibilities of life. Once they begin to dream – then own – their dream, their life changes. Each breath is a gift – each heartbeat – each though – each opportunity to learn, grow and relate. For most it is a rebirth – a second change – a reaffirmation of life and their life. It can be that way.

~~~~~~~~~~

Presence in the Present

Take a minute and think about the present – your present – the time right now that you are living through. It is a most amazing experience – this 'present' that is yours and yours alone. It's not the 'world's present' or 'humanities' present' but yours alone. No other person will ever have the privilege of living through it. It is truly and uniquely yours alone.

And what can you do with this immediate now? I urge you to think carefully about this question. It is here for you right now and, when it's gone, it will be forever gone. At the core of every human experience is this immediacy. Some people think of it as the 'terrible urgency of now' but I suggest that you try to receive it as the 'delightful serendipity of now'. Perhaps there is some benefit in the 'darker' interpretation but I hope you might have trouble seeing it against the truly amazing opportunity that chance and circumstance has given you.

Think about this present that has presented itself to you. What could you do with it that would make it worth having lived through? You could experience it intensely, grow emotionally or intellectually, reach out beyond the narrow range of your life, connect with a feeling that is new, gain inspiration from others or yourself – or you could let it pass into the deep mist of history unrequited – unfulfilled.

You see the present that has been given to you is a gift – unsolicited and non-returnable. It is yours for the briefest of times – yours and yours alone. There has never been nor never shall be its equal.

Zen Buddhism teaches that living in the present means experiencing it without comment – directly as the person living through it rather than as an observer of someone living through it. Buddhism teaches that the way to connect directly with your present is to connect with the immediacy of your 'now'. For instance, you can concentrate on your breathing – quiet your mind and let the rest of the world drop away until there is only the experience of your lungs filling then emptying. The journey to meditation can begin with such a focus. You may never feel more truly alive than when you are experiencing such things as your own breathing.

You can use this present to grow emotionally. Beethoven's titanic struggle with despair and soaring affirmation of hope – the 9th Symphony – can inspire and lead you to understand that it is not so much the hand that you are dealt which matters as how you play it out. Listening to that magnificent composition is to sit within the mind and experience firsthand a human response that turned from the despair of circumstance to the wonder of life. If a composer who lived by his hearing can address the despair of going deaf and push through that despair to write the Ode to Joy, why can't you do the same in your own way? The present is a beacon – a path forward – that only needs taking. Despair is a wasted response to the opportunity to feel the joy of being alive.

You can reach out beyond the narrow range that your life has become. I remember doing this when I decided – quite on impulse – to take up kayaking. Something in me said 'get out on the water' – so I did. The first time out I realized how much I had been missing. Gliding across the water in that diminutive craft – powered only by myself – feeling myself merge with the rhythm of the water and the kayak – experiencing the closeness of nature – all of this came to me because I reached beyond where I was to a new experience. Each time I go out the present becomes alive for me. You can do the same. Maybe it's not kayaking for you but something else that makes your life more than it was. That is the opportunity that your present brings – the gift of living within it.

The present may be an opportunity to experience a feeling intensely – to connect with some part of you that has been neglected. In some ways this is like visiting a too long neglected part of a garden and deciding on a whim to spent time making up for that neglect. Sometimes life doesn't allow us to visit those more remote places within us – but that is often where the most rewarding parts of our life are waiting to be discovered.

Sometimes the present conspires to bring you an opportunity to connect with others in ways that inspire or help you grow in new directions. Remember that your present is often well populated with such opportunities. As transient as they may seem on the surface, these chances can be doorways to very rich and deep places deep within your living experience. I am often amazed at the results of chance encounters – enduring results that contribute richly to my life.

All of these and more – are opportunities that you have within the now that is your present. These precious gifts should not be lost to inattention – they should be savored with a relish that befits them. No one else can live your present because no one will ever be given the opportunity. The life that you have is uniquely yours and the time that comes with it will pass away whether you savor it or not. The only real choice you have is how you will live it.

~~~~~~~~~~~

Wondering Why?

Many of my mentoring engagements begin with a focus on the kinds of questions that a client has been asking themselves. It may seem strange at first to suggest that it is the question rather than the answer which is important; but that is the case more often than not. The seminal indicator that this is the case is the 'why' question.

- Why is this happening to me?
- Why am I so unlucky?
- Why does everybody treat me this way?
- Why can't I live a life that I enjoy?
- Why can't I find my true calling?

It takes a lot of heavy lifting to get a client to see that their questions are really the first challenge that we have to attack. We have to replace all those questions with 'how' questions.

- How can I change what is happening to me?

- How can I become luckier?

- How can I get everybody to treat me with respect and kindness?

- How can I live a life that I will enjoy?

- How can I find my true calling?

The simple change from why to how brings a fundamental shift in the way each client sees themselves. The why questions are for victims while the how questions are for people who are pro-active in molding their life. When you begin to figure out how to make your life better, you have taken a major step forward. Once you give up the status of victim and become the author of your own life, you begin to create that life rather than having others create it for you.

This simple change can bring a major shift in a client's self-image. It can also radically change their behavior. I sometimes feel as if I have turned a precocious two-year-old loose in the world. But now, instead of why, the persistent question is how? One client rushed up to me in a restaurant and said, "My life has completely changed. Now every experience becomes a how question. I am always looking for ways to make my life better. I always am asking myself, how I can make it better."

Always take care of your life; never let it become an accident already happening.

~~~~~~~~~

Ways and Whys of Talking

Ever eavesdrop on a couple of people talking? Sure, we all have. I started to do a lot of that a while back – just to see if there were patterns. I wasn't interested so much in what was being said but how and why it was being said. What I found was fascinating. When people talk there almost always seems to be one of two broad structures to their conversation. These two patterns of 'talk' are quite different and seem to grow out of agreed upon assumptions about the purpose of their talking.

Information Transfer

The first reason people seem to talk is to impart information. I will be telling you something that I believe you didn't know and, presumably, which you either want to or need to know. In this kind of 'talking' the exchange is unidirectional – from the informed to the uninformed – with the 'transaction' resulting in you being better informed. You will notice that I did not choose words that suggested any relationship between what I was telling you and either fact or truth. This kind of 'talk' is proselytizing and is a process of instruction.

Sometimes this exchange is two-way – but within the same pattern. I will tell you something that I suspect you didn't know then it's your turn to tell me something that you suspect that I didn't know. This kind of 'conversation' often reminds me of a tennis game – when the ball arrives on your side of the net you have 'received' – then it's your turn and you return fire – sending your gift of enlightenment back over the net. The pattern continues until an errant shot takes the ball outside the boundaries of the court.

Tennis is a good example for another reason – social distancing is a big part of 'type of talk'. Participants see themselves as separate from each other and engaged in a process that is inherently both linear and binary – involving distinctly defined roles and prerogatives. I've noticed three variations on this pattern:

The Lecture: In this situation it is mutually accepted that one of the participants is far better informed than the other and bears the responsibility to 'educate the other. In this variation the objective is the transfer of information with the results that the 'student's' beliefs becoming more closely aligned with the 'instructor's'. Most proselytizers prefer to adopt this stance – although sometimes the audience doesn't go along with the proposed arrangement.

The Debate: Here two or more people engage in a process designed to achieve ascendancy for their particular views. An organized debate can seem very much like a tennis match – with both sides lobbing their most potent weapons at the other – trying to impress the judge – whether that judge is an individual or the 'public' – that their position should be considered best. Here the objective is to dominate the other side and have your position prevail. A good example of this kind of communication is the back and forth 'war of words' engaged in by political hacks. This kind of communication is inherently tribal – driven by the proposition that the fortunes of a subset of humanity – for instance, the Democratic or Republican Party – is the most important issue – it's the tribe against the rest of the world. These kinds of debates take on the dynamics of artillery duels with the civilian population considered little more that background noise – irrelevant bystanders. Debates are not about seeking the truth – they are about winning.

The Competition: In a competition the principal objective is to win – the details of the position become secondary to the 'game'. The objective becomes the 'most effective advocacy' or, to put it in post-modernist terms 'lobbying'. Most of the practitioners of this form of talking are hired guns – lawyers, lobbyists, politicians or talk show hosts (my somewhat derisive terms for what passes for TV journalists these days). You get paid so you argue for your client's position. You're an actor and suddenly some soap becomes the best thing since sliced bread. You are a lobbyist and suddenly toxic waste is really not that toxic at all.

Once you start looking for them, you can find examples of all three of these 'patterns'. They are dominant in the media simply because television and most radio programming are mono-directional. But, if you listen to most talk radio or watch most TV interview shows (the ones where the talking heads are not just interviewing each other), you will also see lots of examples of the tennis match approach to 'talking'.

The overall defining characteristic of these types of 'talking' is that somebody wins – that one side prevails – that one person comes around to see it from another's perspective. As a result the conversations are mostly a zero sum – I have been proven right and you have been proven wrong – or as a net plus one event – you were against now you are neutral. Of course, the grand objective of all this type or 'talking' is the net plus two result – you are now essentially me on this issue – we agree completely.

Construction Projects

The second pattern is something that I call the construction project. There is a different dynamic in this form of talking – and a great difference in the purpose of the conversation. The first – and most important – difference is the emergence of a middle ground – a space between which comes to be used as a kind of drafting table. Envision it this way – you and I are sitting at a table and on it there is a project that we are working on. We are working to improve it – figure out how to make it work better. Our focus is on the project and we both are involved in contributing ideas – making suggestions – as to how it can be improved. Maybe following your idea, we change it this way and try it out. Then, following my suggestions we try it another way and see how that goes. In the end it is the impact of the changes – the impact on the project – that determines how useful either of our contributions has been.

This is clearly a much more complex process of communication. I need to communicate my ideas so clearly that you actually understand what I am proposing – and are able to see the implications of my suggestions. This is a far more difficult task than the one which arises out of the first type of communication where my proselytizing only has to convert you to my point of view – even if you don't understand its complete implications. Because we are building something between us – an understanding or a design for something that we will build – or something that we are actually building – my dedication needs to be to the project – to what is evolving in the space between us.

I also need to be able to rely on you for the same approach. Without an agreement on this essential point, our conversation will take on a distorted shape and the space and project between us will be replaced by an empty void – proselytizing will become our only remaining recourse.

This type of communication is inherently collaborative. In fact, there is something conspiratorial – in the mildest meaning of the word – about such 'talking'. Participation need to be guided by the ideals of contribution and construction of a common vision. And as we talk – and stay firmly dedicated to the principals of collaboration, contribution and constructiveness – we see the cumulative results of our efforts rising before your eyes – something that was not there before we started. This is a process of creation.

One of the major differences between 'instructive' and 'constructive' communication is the net result – the objective is fundamentally different. Whereas 'instructive' communicators will settle for results ranging from zero to a paltry plus two, the 'constructive' communicators are focused on results that vastly exceed plus two – why not plus 100 or plus 1000?

I have noticed three variations on this pattern of 'talking':

Equal but different: In this variation two people – one lyricist and another a composer for example – collaborate to write a new song. In an increasingly complex world where multi-disciplinary approaches are necessary to solve complex problems, these kinds of partnerships are essential. The objective is agreed on – the contributions are made by each party – the thing grows between them – and the value of their efforts is determined by how well each made their contributions – and how well they combined their individual skills and knowledge to create the results. If nobody ever sings or plays the song, what was the point?

Hierarchical but not: Imagine an operating room – an operation is taking place – there is the surgeon and the support staff – various specialists – nurses. Each brings a skill to the operation – each makes a contribution to the hoped for results. The project is there on the operating table – the patient. The objective is to relieve the project of some 'inconvenience'. Each participant in the 'conversation' has a skill – a role – a technology to bring to bear. Now it is not just a lyricist and composer – but a broader range of skills and capabilities that collaborate towards a common objective.

Facilitation: Sometimes it is important to have a third party occupy the middle ground with the project. This facilitation is in some ways similar to the function of an air traffic controller – assuring an orderly arrival and consideration of the contributions or the various parties to the conversation. In another way a facilitator is like a compass – keeping things pointing in the right direction and assuring that the overall objectives of the conversation are kept front and center. A facilitator can also be a dispassionate determiner of merit when disagreements arise. Think of this form of talking as refereed collaboration.

All of these variations begin with the same thing – and agreement on the purpose of the 'talk' – on the project that is to be addresses. That is the central difference between the two forms – 'instructive' and 'constructive'. I have moderated – facilitated – conversations during some of my consulting engagements – and, in doing so pushed the idea that an agreement on purpose should precede discussions of differences. The results most often were a morphing of the dynamics from an instructive to construction model.

Collaborative communication can result in significant multiplier effects – massive increases in the combined impacts of the various skills and knowledge available within the team. Because personal score-keeping does not dominate the process, the results can be significantly greater.

A tap on the shoulder

Here is something that you can do that may help you see the patterns of 'talking' that you gravitate towards – and to assess the impact – or cost – or those patterns. Take a small blank card and write 'instructive' on one side and 'constructive' on the other. Keep it hands – somewhere you might find it by a chance action. I put mine in my right pocket because I have a habit of putting my hand there while talking. When you do 'happen upon' the card, take it out an look at it – turn it over and ask yourself which of the two you are adopting and is that adoption helping or hurting your overall objective in talking to this person. These 'taps on the shoulder' can help bring you in contact with your behaviors and help you improve your communication skills and the results that come from them.

<u>Finding Meaning Without Manufacturing Meaning</u>

The human tendency to label – and call the label the meaning of the thing – can prevent us from experiencing the world as we find it. Insisting that the meaning of something is what we say it is is rather like shouting loudly at somebody that is trying to tell us something important and then insisting what we were shouting was their real message.

~~~~~~~~~~~~~~~~~~~

The search for meaning is one of life's continuing journeys. The suspicion that meaning is lacking can bring on a deep dread that can haunt us all. The dreary landscape of the suspicion of no meaning can lead us to make up meaning. Buddhists call this ornamentation – the creation of bright and pretty things to enliven the world as think we find it. But the world we think we find is often a world we dream while asleep.

Ornaments are synthetic realities. When we attribute meaning to an event or an idea we are expressing dissatisfaction with things as we think they are. Some of these ornaments play important roles in our lives – and make them better. We believe, for instance, that time is a river flowing from then through now to the future. That vision of time allows us to be 'on time' for meetings and know when to eat, sleep and go to work. Of course, time is nothing like that – but the ornament helps us organize our life.

Other ornaments distance us – give us a false sense of security – and keep us from experiencing important truths. We imagine, for instance, that there is such a time as our 'self' and then see the world in 'self-centric' terms. As a result, we see our self as separate from the rest of the world – isolated in the body which we call ours. This ornament can cause great melancholy and sometimes deep depression.

There is a difference between understanding and explaining. Ornaments explain – often without the requisite understanding. Understanding can free us from a reliance on ornaments.

Perhaps an example might help. Think about something you do regularly during your day. It doesn't have to be a major thing – in fact, is will be easier if it's something you do without thinking. Maybe it's meditation or brushing your teeth. Perhaps doing the dishes or taking a walk. Now think about why you do it – why you began doing it and why you still do it.

I take a walk nearly every day. At first, I started walking for the exercise – the noble idea that I was doing something for my life. Treadmills bored me and their suggestions about the nature of modern life are discomforting. But walking was different. There was movement – new places to see – a world that was not virtual – unpredictable events and occasionally meeting fellow travelers along the way – I enjoy the occasional conversation with a deer, raccoon or squirrel. A while back I started to think about walking and why I walked. The conclusion I came to surprised me. Walking had no purpose – no meaning – outside of walking. The purpose of walking was walking. Walking was just that – walking.

What changed was how I thought of walking – the ornament that I attached to it was gone. It was no longer a matter of covering five or six miles in order to exercise for a couple of hours – extend my life, strengthen my heart. Something had changed. I suspect it started when I discovered the tow path along the C&O Canal here in Washington. It is a delightful opportunity to walk through interesting countryside – with the constant seduction of side-paths through the woods and along the river. The exploration started with the part of the path nearest home but gradually extended to a park around Great Falls. There I found dozens of trails and much to explore.

I realized that there was now something different about walking. At the start, I wanted to see it as exercise – to overcome my resistance to exercising in order to exercise. The meaning of walking was exercise. I wanted walking to be something more than it was and so I turned it into an ornament and called the ornament the 'meaning of walking'. Like everybody else, I wanted all parts of my life to have meaning – to have the things I do have meaning. I wanted to avoid meaningless. I wanted to have a story to tell about how I covered six miles yesterday and felt so good as a result. Now I realize how foolish that effort is.

Meaning is – it's not manufactured. Pretending to live is not living authentically. Living to pretend is living to avoid living. Being present in the present is the antidote to an addiction to living with ornaments.

We all want our lives to have meaning. The human ability to envision a time when we are no more – when we can no longer remind people we are – infects us with a dread of that time when we are no more and nobody remembers that we were here. In quiet moments we may chide ourselves for being less than we can be and for doing meaningless things. In the weak moments that follow we take to constructing ornaments.

The big ornament on this tree is a proposed 'coherent narrative' of some sort that we weave around the idea of our 'self' – a narrative in which we are separate from the rest of the universe. We tell ourselves a story of our 'self' and then insist that that 'self' has meaning. But the truth is that we don't exist as a 'self' with meaning but as living human beings. Any meaning beyond that is manufactured. We do not represent something else. Each of us is here in their own right. As a human being, just as with a lion or a rock, we are complete meaning without ornaments.

Maybe another example will help.

Meditation is. Neither good nor bad – easy nor hard – advanced nor beginner meditation is simply meditation. Doing meditation means meditating – not 'improving yourself' – nor seeking enlightenment – nor proving superiority – meditation is simply meditation. Like breathing or a bowel movement, it is sufficient to itself and no manufactured meaning makes it more than that.

This tends to be a very hard idea for many who see meditation in ornamented terms. I remember listening to a lecture on meditation during which the teacher made exactly this point. One in the audience became quite upset at the idea. *"I thought that meditation was the path to enlightenment. You say that it is not a path to anywhere – just something you do. What do I get out of meditating? You seem to be saying 'nothing'. Then why should I meditate?"*

The meaning of meditation is in meditating. Adding the ornament of 'something to gain by meditating' introduces the idea of grasping – an ornament – into the process. "I meditate to gain enlightenment" is a manufactured meaning that 'overwrites' the true meaning.

Like most of what we do in life, meditation isn't about anything other than meditation – meditation is simply meditation. If you try to define it in terms of something, you confuse the issue and insulate yourself from experiencing the meaning of meditation. The experience of the ornament becomes a substitute for direct experience. At that point, something destructive occurs. Meditation becomes like every other self-improvement system.

What would you have your meditation mean? Should it get closer to god, help you 'find yourself', or maybe enrich your life or circumstances. You don't need to meditate for all that. There are plenty of therapists, self-help books, and programs to provide distractions from direct experience. They thrive on the idea that your life can be adjusted – brought into focus – their focus – and, thereby, filled with meaning – their meaning. It seems to me that meditation is – if nothing else – an oasis – a refuge from all of that. It is a way to drop all the ornaments and just be – just breathe – and to let meaning emerge.

I remember sitting in a small forest clearing some years back. A warm rock in a sunny spot was too inviting to ignore. When I first sat down, there were no animals to be seen but, as I sat quietly, they began to appear – the clearing became full of life. Less is truly more. Direct experience of the present is possible only when we clear away all intervening ornaments – only when we experience it directly.

91

Meditation is precisely the opposite of ornamentation. It isn't repairing and adjusting – striving and wanting things to be different – it is settling into an experience of things as they are without overwriting them with our 'editorial tendencies'. Mastering that simple idea can bring thunderous changes to your experience of living and meaning. Now meditation requires neither effort nor discipline – it is neither hard nor easy – it is as you can do it and no more. If you experience meditation – and anything else in your life – that way, you will enter the world as it is and experience the joy that replaces the guilt – guilt that ornamentation always brings.

When you meditate – meditate and nothing more. When you walk – walk and nothing more. When you live – live and nothing more. The meaning in all these is more than all the meaning you might manufacture.

There are more things in heaven and earth, Horatio, than are dreamt of in your philosophy. Hamlet, Act 1, Scene V

Meditation, walking and living can be a refuge from the world of self-improvement, personal guilt and ornamentation. When everything else is something it is not, they can be simply what they are. A life of ornamentation is struggling – striving – worrying that it is not 'just right'. Meditation, walking and living without ornaments is the effortless experience of life as it is.

~~~~~~~~~~

The Missing Middle – Framing the Challenge

When you are facing a vexing challenge, sometimes the best strategy is to get on the phone, gather a brain trust and meet over drinks. These casual and unstructured sessions will often give you the key understandings that will make the challenge far more manageable. It's a simple idea with powerful potential.

~~~~~~~~~~~~~~~~~~~~~~

Whenever I encounter an interesting or particularly vexing problem, I draw together people whose intellect and experience I trust. Over the years I have formed dozens of these 'mission-impossible brain trusts'. They focus on what I consider important issues – particularly ones that have become a burr under my saddle – if you know what I mean. It helps me sort out complex challenges and keeps me from drinking my own bath water. The *quid pro quo* for the team members is that they get fresh thinking on challenges that they may not even have recognized. It tends to be a win-win all around!

The format of these sessions was set long ago – I bring a question of substance – lay it out on the table – everybody takes a first swipe at it – then the floor is open. The rules are simple but enforced. There is no such thing as a bad idea or bad place to start. Every idea is considered – we never want to discard a potentially productive line simply because it was poorly stated or initially described from the wrong angle. So, after the initial forays, the group generally gets down to following each of the approaches. Sometimes sub-groups will break out and with really good questions people start swapping chairs.

These groups are much more productive if populated by experienced hands. But the mix needs to include both conservative and explosive thinkers. And, as moderator, one of my jobs is to make sure that the latter does not charge too far ahead of the former. Balanced dialogue that dives deeply into the challenge put before the group is the objective. Sometimes that is a tough goal to achieve but, for the most part, the group helps me move toward it.

First Round

A while back I organized a discussion group to focus on an issue that had been bothering me. I suspected that some really heavy lifting might be involved so I assembled a particularly serious group – a kind of mission impossible 'A' team. We met for the first time over drinks. There were several current and past CEOs, a VP of Planning, a couple of process consultants and a person who had run a major non-profit. When the group assembled, the question that I placed before them was:

"How do you effectively assure the holistic integration of strategic and tactical planning?"

Everybody's first cut was fairly predictable. There were mutterings about 'optimization' and 'seamless integration'. Lots of focus on the need to make sure that the strategic and tactical plans meshed – grousing about silos and insular perspectives – and more than one reference to this or that system for planning. But, the longer the group talked, the less useful these approaches seemed.

The group quickly realized that the question was far more complex than any of us (including me) had initially assumed. We also came to see that it was a far more important and subtle question than it had seemed on the surface. This was clearly not a question about what kind of dressing you want on your salad. It was more like asking 'what kind of a person do you really want to become and why aren't you becoming that person?'

94

We came to the conclusion that there was a serious flaw in the way the discussions about planning from a holistic perspective were being framed. Interestingly, the consensus quickly developed that this was not so much a question of inadequate process analysis or design. A suggestion was made and accepted that we should focus on the roles of various 'visions' or 'world views' in the overall planning process. This required a return to some very basic issues and the evolution of a new vision. But I am getting ahead of myself.

The initial session ended up with an agreement to work the challenge and to tap into our various resource networks. We agreed to adjourn for a week and try to get as many responses as possible prior to the next session.

I assumed the role of secretary and within seventy-two hours results started pouring in. For my part, I posted the question on Linked In and got a pile of responses. I also circulated it to selected contacts. Other group members were doing the same. By the time the second meeting approached we had some one hundred and sixty-plus pages of comments and suggestions. From the phone and e-mail traffic alone it was clear that we were onto something important.

Round Two

For our second meeting I arranged a large conference room. We were going to need lots of space and fewer distractions. There were at least three slide presentations summarizing data and lots of hand-out materials. As the group assembled I caught a sense of excitement in the air. Intense conversations flared up here and there – people became animated during them.

I called the meeting to order and outlined the ground rules. Our first objective was to present findings – no rush to conclusions until all the data was on the table. So during the next hour or so each member in turn displayed their 'haul'. Much of it was similar to our initial, discarded focus but every now and then a more 'global' vision would show its face.

After the presentations, the group decided to focus on and rough out that 'global' vision. It was an important step that allowed the insights that came. Our general agreement was:

> *'Let's not focus on the planning process – everybody does that – let's think about holistic planning from a global resourcing rather than a structure and process point of view'.*

This focus was based on a widely held suspicion. The group was concerned that starting at any point in the process would taint our approach to other parts. The research for my PhD thesis came into play. I had worked to develop an alternative to comparative cultural analysis – the rub here being that every comparison is done by someone in one of the cultures being compared – and you can guess how that informs their conclusions.

As a group, we were determined to avoid the ideology of particular disciplines or cultural biases. Early on I had introduced a quote from Lotfi Zadeh (the father of fuzzy logic):

> *"When all you have is a hammer, everything starts to look like a nail".*

The Question Restated

The group went back to the original question and started to rework it. The idea was to try to frame it in such a way that a focus on the 'global vision' would naturally be forced front and center. By deciding to think about the resourcing rather than the structure of the process the group adopted the military maxim:

> *Amateurs talk about tactics – professionals focus on logistics. And, in this case the group decided, logistics begins with the question of 'vision' resourcing.*

We began to think about the resources (visions or world-views) that had to be present (both quantitatively and qualitatively) if planning was to have any chance to be 'holistically integrated from the strategic to the tactical'. The general consensus was that there were certain components that had to be present if planning was to have any chance of being productive and effectively integrated front to back.

But there was something else in play as well – a shadow focus. The group had also begun to think about the enormous costs of provincial or 'faux-holistic' planning. In a fevered diversion, we took turns describing how a minor error in judgment or a lack of consideration of this or that critical issue could set the entire process off on a very non-productive direction.

This idea was highlighted by a group member who had recently had a very expensive car stop operating because of a failure of a small and rather inexpensive part – which it turned out, was poorly engineered. In complex systems, the failure of apparently non-critical parts can have catastrophic effects.

So now the sub-question became:

What were the conditions a priori that could increase the chances of success for a holistic planning process?

Logistics first – then strategy and tactics! As a first step we tried to find the knots at the two ends of the 'rope'

The Knots at the Ends of the Rope – Visionaries and Theater Commanders

The conversation took a decisive turn when we agreed that there were at least two fundamentally different understandings of the world implied by the restated question. The first we labeled the 'strategic view' or the 'view from 60,000 feet' while the second became the 'theater commander's view' or the 'view from 6,000 feet'. We agreed to work under the assumption that these were the major terminal 'nodes' in the process.

We first considered the 'view from 60,000 feet'. Our first

97

effort was to identify people who were successful practitioners in it space. Most of them are called either futurists or visionaries. We discarded the former and decided on the latter because a suggestion was made that there were people who, by focusing on the past, were visionaries for the future. Many names were bandied about. Some of them were Gene Roddenberry, Alvin and Heidi Toffler, Henry Kissinger, Buckminster Fuller, Isaac Asimov, Margaret Mead, B.F. Skinner, Nicholas Negroponte, Arthur C. Clarke, Bill Gates, Warren Buffett, Newton, Einstein and Descartes.

We decided to apply a set of screens to help identify those 'visionaries' who had, or currently were, providing insights that would be useful in driving the process of holistic business planning. This turned out to be much more of a challenge than we had first thought. The question quickly became 'is apparent relevance or demonstrated accuracy more important'? In other words, when you are betting on the future, would you follow the lead of a 'visionary' that seemed to be making sense within what you understood to be the current trends (even if they were mostly unproven as a seer) or would you go with another who is saying things that only marginally make sense but who has a history of being right when it comes to identifying serious disruptive shifts or abrupt course changes?

The group decided to bet on the latter – primarily because we considered the problem of 'faux visionaries' or 'legends in their own minds'. This decision lead us to require that, in order to qualify as a true 'visionary', a person would need to have a track record of being right and a reputation for truly independent thinking. Keep in mind that we were working on the problem of designing a holistic approach to planning that would effectively integrate the strategic and the tactical. Our judgment was that if the process did not begin with a truly visionary understanding of the advancing world, the process was going to be fundamentally flawed.

Two degrees off course and you miss paradise and sail off

into the vastness of the open ocean!

All of the people that we initially named were proven sources of insight into the likelihood of this or that new development becoming the new norm. But in order to arrive at the true 'upper end of the rope' we decided to think in terms proposed by Thomas Kuhn in The Structure of Scientific Revolutions. For those of you who haven't read it, Kuhn observed that *"a scientific community cannot practice its trade without some set of received beliefs."* Further he suggested that these beliefs form the foundation of an "educational initiation that prepares and licenses the student for professional practice".

Normal Science, according to Kuhn, *"is predicated on the assumption that the scientific community knows what the world is like"* and scientists take great pains to defend that assumption.

In contrast to 'normal science', Kuhn defined a 'scientific revolution' as *"a non-cumulative developmental episode in which an older paradigm is replaced in whole or in part by an incompatible new one"*. He suggested that a scientific revolution that results in paradigm change is analogous to a political revolution that results in an entirely new form of government.

The group agreed that those individuals who have a proven capability to anticipate and accurately describe advancing 'paradigm shifts' were the ones we were looking for.

One thing we easily agreed on is that it takes years of thinking and re-thinking about the world from a global perspective to develop an even passably useful strategic vision. There are thinkers who focus on this level and, over many years, develop a sure grasp of the likely direction and intentionality of global systems. Most of them dedicate their lives to the process and the good ones operate without an ideological agenda. The group agreed that such animals are rare and could name only about a dozen that might qualify.

Another quick agreement was on the danger of too loosely defining a paradigm shift. Those of us who had read Kuhn's striking introduction to the second edition of his book remember well his regret over the misuse of the term paradigm. It got so, at least according to some pundits, that there were several paradigm shifts every day. As a friend of mine was fond of observing, *"A paradigm here and a paradigm there and you are still a couple of nickels short of half a dollar! Paradigms should be made of sterner stuff."* So we decided to be purist about it and adopt Kuhn's proffered narrow definition – "When paradigms change, the world itself changes with them".

Clearly the group was now focusing on a specific kind of planning – one that attempted to look 'over the horizon' and 'beyond the logical implications of currently known trends'. We realized that our focus had become similar to that of the senior management teams of trans-global companies and national governments. The planning we were now talking about strove to anticipate, mitigate the disruptive effects of and, if possible, take advantage of the displacements caused by highly disruptive paradigm shifts.

With the definition of 'visionary' fairly well roughed out, the group shifted focus to the knot at the other end of the rope. The second world view – 'view from 6,000 feet'- was seen as being far more ideologically proscribed and certainly based on the concepts of normal science. These were managers of practitioners of a very wide range of 'normal sciences'. If the 'visionary' was the architect then the 'theater commander' was the construction project supervisor. Their troops are people who are trained in specific disciplines – following established procedures and applying, within strict limits, what Thomas Kuhn referred to as 'normal science'.

To be clear, the group decided to focus a bit back from the very end of the rope – the platoon-level foot troops that make up the front-lines of any implementation effort. The theater commanders were interesting to us because they managed a widely divergent set of resources and skill-sets that had to be closely coordinated. These individuals ran large and complex operations mostly on a virtual basis.

Much like the 'visionaries', the group agreed that these theater commanders took a very long time to mature. Although they may have begun their careers in a single discipline, their contribution to the process was the identification, evaluation, deployment and management of a wide range of resources in order to implement a complex plan targeted towards achieving extraordinary results. It takes years of experience to develop these capabilities.

One thing the group found very interesting about theater commanders is that they seemed to be the first major node along the rope whose focus is predominately virtual. By that we meant that they assemble teams of experts across a very side range of disciplines – most of which focus in well-defined bodies of 'received knowledge' – but their own expertise is in the management of these diverse disciplines.

A group member suggested that the theater commanders were very much like very accomplished translators – a kind of uber-translator. They represented the first 'focus node' – meaning that they transmitted the orders, requirements, schedules, etc. down the line – translating them into 'local speak' in the process. They also communicated results, failures, anomalies, unexpected challenges, etc. back up the line and into 'strategic-speak' in the process.

Oil and Water

Once we had agreed on the distal nodes of the planning process, the group turned to considering how well these distinct world views collaborate. It quickly became apparent that the distance between the two was creating some fairly aberrant behaviors in an attempt to bridge the gap.

Purveyors of each world view regularly attempt to adopt the perspective and behavior of the other. Architects occasionally pick up a hammer and theater commanders attempt to think like generals – usually with disappointing results in both cases.

There was a sense that, among theater commanders, the strategic vision had to be an integral part of the planning process – but an inadequate structure and resourcing to make it so. Many of these 'reinvention-out-of-necessity' attempts were clearly visible in mid-size and larger consulting firms. Consultants had established advisory boards of 'visionaries' to try to bring the 'truly visionary' into their practice. Others had simply adopted this or that world-view and become 'forceful advocates' for it. In most cases the results were simply a consulting firm with a gimmick.

Some members of the group were also familiar with 'visionaries' who had started a consulting firm to help translate their visions into practicable knowledge. Several came to mind almost immediately. The one which we focused the most attention on was Kissinger Associates, the New York City-based international consulting firm founded by Henry Kissinger. Here was a 'visionary' who had founded a company to advise clients on strategic issues and help them plan for advancing paradigm shifts.

The discussion focused on the personal history of Dr. Kissinger – in an effort to establish why he was able to accomplish what many others found so difficult. Something important came out of that part of the discussion.

The group agreed that there is no linear progression from one world view to the other. In other words, a very experienced theater commander does not very often evolve into a strategic visionary and a visionary does not very often become an effective theater commander.

The training is different – the accumulated experience is different as well – and the required knowledge and patterns of thought are radically different. "It would be like arguing that if you increased your proficiency in English enough you would suddenly start speaking French", one member observed. And, though the nit-pickers among us would have liked to pull apart the metaphor, we agreed that the preserved truth was more important than the ego exercises on offer. The lesson in all of this was quite clear:

A marlin cannot fly and an eagle cannot live under water. That does not make the marlin less because it is not an eagle or the eagle greater because it is not a marlin. Both are necessary to the process – both are important to the extent that they are potent as who they are.

Inherent Schizophrenia

Roses are red, violets are blue
I'm schizophrenic and so am I

By the time the session began to wind down, it was apparent that we were focused on a highly complex and subtle process that, in order to be reliably effective, had to find some way of integrating two radically divergent world perspectives. If a planning process which focused 'over the horizon' was to function holistically, there needed to be a bridge across the chasm – a unifying mechanism.

I recalled part of an interview that I had seen with John Forbes Nash Jr., the math prodigy who was able to solve problems that had baffled the greatest minds. He overcame years of suffering through schizophrenia and eventually won the Nobel Prize. When asked how he overcame his schizophrenia, his response was *"I became disillusioned with my delusions"*.

By the end of the session the group was focused on the question "how do you design, resource and manage a consulting firm that is able to holistically translate the visionaries insights into actionable advice for a client?"

The coffee was gone, schedules had been mangled and people were tired. But they were also game to continue in a follow-on session to deal with that question.

~~~~~~~~~~

Leaving the Rut Means Growing Your Life

An old friend was fond of observing the "*a person needs to be repotted every few years*". A bit of living has shown me how much wisdom there is in that simple statement. All of us have the same experience at times. We realize that we have settled into a rut and wonder how we came to be there. Sometimes the realization comes on quickly and at other times it seems that years have passed before we realize. But there comes a time when we begin to sense that we need to break out of patterns that have dominated our lives. It is time to leave the rut behind and strike out in a new direction. We feel the need to be repotted.

Of course, realizing and doing are two very different things. The realizing can bring on a sense of shame at what we have allowed to happen to our life. This can be a mind killer if you let it. The experience can be very humbling. The most poignant description of that experience is a poem by Antonio Machado titled '*The Wind One Brilliant Day*'.

The wind one brilliant day called to my soul with an odor of jasmine.

"In return for the odor of my jasmine, I'd like all the odor of your roses."

"I have no roses; all the flowers in my garden are dead."

"Well then, I'll take the withered petals and the yellow leaves and the waters of the fountain."

And the wind left. And I said to myself: *"What have you done with the garden that was entrusted to you?"*

It does not have to be that way, but sometimes we neglect our garden. And suddenly we are reminded by a passing wind how much damage we have allowed. For most of us, that is the call to action. The question is, once you come to realize how much tending your garden needs, how you react.

The garden in Machado's poem is your life. You are the gardener and its condition is your responsibility. The flowers are your relationships and the things you are doing with the time and energy you have been given. The first, and essential step, is to realize that it does not have to be that way. You can better tend your garden and make it a wonderland of intoxicating odors and splashes of colors. It is really up to you and each action you take will either being it to life or condemns it to dreariness.

So, let us say that you have reached that point in your life. It is time to begin gardening in earnest. How do you go about it? There are a few important steps you can take. Most of them relate to how you see yourself and the role you can play in creating your own life. Here are a few suggestions:

Clear away the Dead Things: Ruts are constructed of things that limit your possibilities and cause frustration and loss of opportunities. Identify those things in your life that are keeping you in the rut. Make a commitment to remove them and clear away the ground so that new plants can be put in their place. Then set about doing just that. Getting out a rut begins with clearing away those things which have created it. You can do it; it is only a matter of making the commitment and following through.

Be Selective about What You Allow in Your Garden: Remember that every part of your life is the way it is, at least in part, because you have accepted its presence. If you have limiting relationships, end them. Replace them with new and more empowering and supportive ones. If you need to develop new skills, decide to develop them and to find the support you need to be successful. Gardening begins with deciding what is, and what is not, going to be allowed to grow.

Be Proactive in Your Gardening: Remember that gardening is all about taking care of the things you have planted. If you want to experience that directly, go out and do some actual gardening. I am serious about this. Find a plot of ground or a large flowerpot and make it into a garden. There is nothing quite as uplifting as seeing things grow under your care. It will bring you into contact with a wisdom that will help you rework you life. Gardening takes consistent attention and skill. Then turn that wisdom loose on your own life. It is really the same skill. You build your own life in much the same way as you build a garden; carefully, methodically and with care and compassion for the things growing in it.

Keep Stagnation Away: Ruts grow like weeds. They are the product of inattention and laziness. Once you become engaged in rebuilding your life, you need to keep at it and take pleasure in every step forward. Do not let your energy and effort lapse. Remember, it took a lot of inattention to get your garden in a sorry state and it will take a lot of consistent effort to turn it into the glorious garden that it can be. Stagnation is a form of death.

Pursue your interests lavishly: Find those things which get your engine revved up and collect them into your life. The richer the mixture, the more vibrant you garden will become.

Celebrate the First Small Steps: When you plant seeds, nothing much seems to happen for a while. But the real miracle of life is going on even when you cannot see it. Soon there will be the first green shoots poking up through the soil as life reaches for the warmth of the sun. Life is that way if it is allowed to grow under the right conditions. Your life can be the same. And when it starts to grow, take the time to celebrate.

Have Faith that it Will Flourish: Sure, you can worry that the garden might not end up exactly the way you want it. In truth, it almost never does. Plants have a mind of their own and their own way of being. Things go far better if the gardener does not act as a dictator but as a facilitator. The same is true for your life. You should bring those things into your garden that you want to help grow; and things into your life that will make it more glorious and fulfilling. In neither case will you be able to determine exactly how it will end up, but you can help it grow and enjoy the fruits of your labor anyway.

Have the Courage to be the Gardener: Remember that you are the gatekeeper of your own future. If there are things that are blocking you from fulfilling that role, move them out of the way. Fear or hesitancy is a path that leads back to the rut. Have faith in your own abilities and trust yourself. Every gardener faces this challenge. Every plot of land brings the same challenge. A blank slate is difficult enough, but when you have to clear the land before planting, the initial steps can be daunting. Have faith, roll up your sleeves and get at it. Never become the proverbial deer in the headlights. You can do it, so get cracking and do it.

Keep At It: A garden does not come into full flower at the snap of your fingers. It takes lots of care and consistent attention. The same is true for moving out of a rut and changing your life. It may seem easier to slip back into the stagnation that built the rut, but you need to realize that is a form of death. You are alive precisely to the extent that you are enriching and tending your garden. Give it the life it deserves; the life you deserve.

Now is the Time: Start now. Never wait until you feel up to it. Procrastination is one of the main reasons that you ended up in a rut. The opportunity to start rejuvenating your garden is now. Missing the opportunity is simply staying in that rut.

Take Time to Enjoy the Garden: Remember that you are making the effort and taking the care for a reason. You have decided to make your life more fulfilling. The gardening will help that come to pass. But you need to experience the growth and celebrate it with those close to you. Nothing is more satisfying than showing off your new garden. Let people experience it and your pride of authorship.

Think Ahead and Visualize the New Garden: The work goes better if you have a vision of how your garden will look when it is in full flower. The same is true for your life. Take the time to dream about how much better it will feel to live that new life. Every once in a while stop and look at how things are taking root; then think about how they will look when they are fully grown. If you can see the garden you are trying to grow, you will have a dream that you can work to make come true.

~~~~~~~~~~~~~~~~~~~

If you can begin to see your life as a process, much like the growing garden, you can take the first steps towards making it a reality. If you can dream the garden that you want to grow, you will always have a vision to guide your efforts. If you do both, you are on your way to having the life you deserve.

Breaking Out of a Rut

When I was learning to fish, my father's favorite saying was *"that fish is not going to come towards you unless you turn the handle"*. He usually said that when I was frozen by the shock of having a big fish on the line. Those of you who fish will understand. For those of you who don't, a fishing reel pulls in line when you rotate the handle. Without that action, it is just a curiosity on your end of the fishing pole. To help it to fulfill its purpose, you need to take extended and purposeful action.

Now, let us make somewhat of a leap from fishing reels to real humans. Maybe you have had this experience. You feel that you have been stuck in a rut and are finding it difficult to break out. Maybe you have been there for some time but the awareness is just catching up to you. Perhaps the walls have been closing in a bit more rapidly lately. Or maybe a friend has made a comment that brought your awareness of the rut into sharp relief. What are you going to do about it?

Sure, the easy response is 'climb out of the rut'. But that is often harder to do than say. Think of your rut as a bad personal habit like smoking or drinking to excess. How much easier is it to think about changing those habits than actually changing them? Those of you who have tried know how very difficult it can be. But then what is a rut but just another bad habit?

Seeing the Behavior Rather than the Landscape

One of the reasons that people have such difficulty breaking out of ruts is that they tend to see them as landscape rather than grouped behaviors. It is important to understand the dynamics that are driving the behaviors. In the simplest terms, all ruts are easily left behind if the behaviors which keep us in them vanish. You are not in the rut because it is containing you, the rut is your creation and, as its architect, you have designed, built and maintained it.

Each of these steps (designing, building and maintaining) is the result of behaviors that you adopted mostly without careful thought. They are accidental behaviors. Many of them are self-sabotaging. Maybe they arose because you have a low self-image or lack self-confidence. Maybe your culture, education or family history pushes you in a particular direction. Maybe your peer group insists that these behaviors are part of you. Any or all of these (and more) can be tools that you use to build and maintain your rut.

I Did It to Me

That is the critical realization. You can blame any of the sources of influence but, at some point in your life, you have to take responsibility for your life as you have made it or allowed it to develop. A rut is something you have done to yourself. It does not matter whether the doing was purposeful or negligent. It matters that you are the instrument of your own imprisonment. You fill three roles: jail builder, jailer and prisoner.

This can be a hard thing to realize. It is far easier to find others to blame for your rut. But that hunt is a distraction. Certainly, you are not the architect of your entire life. None of us are. We are born without having given our permission. For most of our early years, we are directed. It is amazing when we do not develop the tendency to see our ruts in terms of what others have done to us. As we mature, there comes a time when blaming others no longer suffices. A sharp cry 'no more' becomes our battle cry. *"I will no longer be the victim in my own life"*.

Charting the Path Out

There is very often a moment like that. You finally come to see that your prison is self-constructed. They you have been your own jailer. Initially there may be a great deal of shame and self-condemnation. *"How could I have done that to myself?"* Then the journey out of the rut can begin. You can begin to chart the course and set your goals. It is the goals that are the key. They give the journey structure and help maintain focus.

First goals are the most important. Keep your eyes on them. It's the ones that you have set near term that will keep you moving forward. Do not make the mistake of focusing on the end goal. It is too far away and you will find it too easy to abandon the journey towards it. Remember that you are trying to change the behaviors that created the rut in the first place. Behaviors take a long time to change. Making the changes a step at a time can help you succeed.

Here are some suggestions that might help:

- Make your goals specific and detailed
- Take small steps at first and then longer ones later on
- Always check your progress and hold yourself

112

accountable

- Goals should be cumulative with the early ones being the solid foundation for the later ones
- Share your goals with people close to you and they will help you meet them
- Celebrate your successes and forgive your failures but redouble your efforts in both cases
- Keep one eye on the end goal and visualize the way you will be and feel once you meet it

Breaking out a rut can be easier if you see it as a behavior change. It can be far easier if you enlist your friends in helping you. In the end, however, it requires your courage and determination to change. Sure a good guide helps. But you are the person who decides *"I will not do that to myself any longer!"*

~~~~~~~~~~

Charting the Course for Change

Most of my mentoring clients come to me with some sort of change in mind. A very few are responding to a general feeling of dissatisfaction. Most want to change something about themselves or their lives. The depth and detail of understanding that they have is one the early indicators of what kind of progress we are going to be able to manage. The more they have come to realize that a change is necessary, the better the progress we will be able to make. The best mentoring engagements begin with specifics and gradually focus on more general issues. Those tend to be the ones with the truly 'eureka' moments. Those are the ones where the lights suddenly go on all over the house and a life is changed forever. Those are the ones that really make mentoring worth the effort.

Initial Sessions

My approach to mentoring begins with a focus on the client and their current situation. A major topic during our first meetings is, 'what do you want to change and why'? You will certainly have at least superficial answers. It may be some limitation on your career. You might describe it as a roadblock that needs to be removed. You may see it as a blind side or character trait that is keeping them from realizing their potential. The common denominators are that 1) you have realized the need to change, and 2) you have sought out my help in making the change. Both are important and affect the likelihood that we will be able to make the important, life-changing progress that all good mentoring engagements should.

The first few mentoring sessions are used to build a baseline. We need to answer the question, 'where are you right now', so that we can plot a course towards where we want to be and also measure our progress along the way. A second part of the process is developing answers to 'where do you want to go, what do you want to change and in what way'. These answers become very useful as time and experience accumulate. They also help us establish a preliminary roadmap complete with milestones and metrics for success. Many clients have kept the assessment results as a reminder of how far they have come since those early sessions. This memento becomes a source of wonder as they think back on the person they were before the changes began.

Two Ends and the Road Between

We will start out with two snapshots frozen in time. The first is the 'where are you right now' baseline while the second is the 'where do you want to go, what do you want to change and in what way' results. After many years of mentoring experience, I have learned that neither snapshot will survive the process intact. One of the main results of our work together will be a much better understanding of both questions and a much more sophisticated answer to each. The first snapshot is really a picture of who you are and what your importance is as a human being in society. Every client I worked with has upped their self-assessment as a result of my mentoring. They come to understand that they have been selling themselves short and underestimating their value. You will do the same. As low self-images begin to fade into the past, they are replaced with brighter and better based one. You will come to have a better understanding of your potential and possibilities. You will substantially raise your expectations and sense of what is possible. Initial understandings are replaced with far more detailed and nuanced ones. In short, the starting point and the end point undergo substantial revisions as we discover the true abilities and possibilities.

Charting the Course – Making the Journey

Once these initial snapshots are in hand, we can begin the real work. We chart a course and develop a strategy to moving along it. Our understanding is specific in terms of success metrics. We need to know if the work is resulting in positive changes and is worth the money and effort that is put into it. But our understanding of the course will change just as the two snapshots will evolve over time.

My mentoring engagement involve an extended weekly session. But it is during the intervening time where the real work is done. Like one of those high school teachers who you wanted to avoid, I give lots of homework! The weekly meetings are to process the results of the homework assignments. This has a double benefit. First, it keeps us from hashing and rehashing the same issues over and over. New fuel is added to the fire and we can move forward with our work. Second, it deepens our discussions while maintaining the focus on our primary objectives; making changes that empower you and add to the potential for a better, more fulfilling and richer life.

I am one to celebrate progress. Each milestone reached, each goal exceeded is an opportunity to recognize the concerted efforts have moved us towards our primary objective. The change that was first sought may have become the redefined change that is now based on a better understanding. The road that we initially thought to follow may have, with a deeper understanding of the possibilities, become a wide and paved superhighway. That is progress as well.

Revising the Charts

During almost two decades of mentoring, I have never had an engagement that ended up exactly following the course initially laid out. Process is essentially self-changing and the course is self-correcting. I'll ask you to keep a journal of our work together. It will be 'exhibit A' in our progress review sessions. Looking back and comparing expectations then with new understandings now will allow us to see the progress that has resulted from our work. This highlights one of the most valuable contributions that mentoring can make to your life. If you understand more of what is there before you, the chances are better that you will make the correct decisions based on a more nuanced reading to the possibilities and limitations. So you see, there are two changes going on. Sure we are moving towards your principal objective. But you also get better at seeing what the journey had to offer. This change is more generally useful as it will apply to many parts of your life. Many of my clients have found this change to be liberating. It can signal a major leap forward and bring much joy and fulfillment into your life.

So, along the way, my clients become map makers. You will learn how to chart a course, think about the best path forward and avoid or plan for challenges that you are going to encounter. You will learn how to distinguish the drivers of change. Sometimes those drivers are a reaction to a need to move away from something. Sometimes they are a need to towards something. You will learn to deal differently with your aversions than your desires. You will also learn how to chart and follow courses that avoid future unwanted problems.

Resting on Your Laurels

One of the truly great experiences in mentoring is to be able to meet with a client as an equal. After the work is done and the goals achieved, after the demons have been slain and the foe vanquished, it is rewarding to pause along life's journey and reflect on the journey made. I relish those times and experiences. Where once there was uncertainty and hesitancy; now there is clarity and resolve. Where once there was fear and loathing; now there is confidence and compassion. Moving forward means growing. Growing means maturing. Maturity means having the luxury to rest a bit and contemplate the wonder of life before embarking on the next great quest.

~~~~~~~~~~

Apprehension – Fear or Understanding?

Thinking about the meanings of word can often lead to a better understanding of our view of the world and place in it. I don't mean debating the meanings in the dictionary – I mean discovering which of two definitions you prefer and why. Self-knowledge can be increased by acknowledging linguistic preferences.

~~~~~~~~~~~~~~~~~~~~

Language can be a complicated thing – particularly when it comes to those curious words that have multiple meanings. It's not so much the existence of the meanings that intrigues me but the choices that people make. How a person chooses to use a particular word can tell you a great deal about who they are and how they see the world and their place in it. Take, for instance, the word 'apprehension'. I've noticed that few people actually use the word – perhaps because of the complex of meanings that surround it – but, when it is used, it generally is deployed in description of a situation. Let's start with three definitions:

- **fearful expectation or anticipation**: "the man looked around the dark alley with apprehension"

- **understanding**: the cognitive condition of someone who understands; "he has a solid understanding of the situation and its implications"

- **the act of apprehending** (especially apprehending a criminal): "the policeman on the beat got credit for the collar"

That is a wide range on meanings for one word. Now take a minute to reflect on the meaning which you attach to the word. It is probably a good idea to spend some time thinking this through. I am sure that your natural inclination is to opt for the meaning that has the highest positive loading. But, and here is the rub, the real question is how you face the world as you find it and which of the meanings tend to dominate your approach.

It will be easy to think of this exercise as a 'word game' – multiple choices with a single right answer. That's not going to get to the nub of this. You see, your tendencies are at the core of how you see yourself and the world around you – and (this is the important part) how you see the people around you. Maybe three examples might help.

Mentoring and Personal Growth I work with senior executives, entrepreneurs and members of boards. They tend to be very well educated and have a complex understanding of language – they are good at it and being good at it allows them to be successful. But it also presents traps that are hard to avoid and very difficult to escape from.

• **Bob's Story**: A while back I had a mentoring engagement with a CEO (let's call him Bob) who is building his second business. Early on I noticed that he had a well-defined approach to major challenges – he avoided them as long as possible. When I first directed his attention to that habit, he reacted strongly and negatively to the suggestion. He was, after all, a leader and founder of two businesses.

The first evidence of his tendency came when he had to terminate a senior member of his team. The relationship had a considerable history but it was clear that this person was not producing. Bob avoided confronting the problem even as it caused more damage to the potential of his business and increased tensions among other members of the team. Our sessions got tenser until one day Bob exploded. The emotions came flooding out. "I can't change the team. Think of all the bad things that might happen." When I asked him to describe those 'bad things', he began to outline the likely reactions of the team member. "He might sue us or cause the company to fall apart." Bob was apprehensive about making the change – the negatives of having to take the action were all he was seeing.

A while later we began to focus on a part of Bob's personal life that was heading for a crisis. The behavior was much the same. He avoided making decisions – taking any action – until things approached the boiling point. I pointed out the similarity of the pattern. This time – and in the light of the other issue – he was far less dismissive. As he described his dilemma and tried to rationalize his approach to it, it became clear that he was again focused on the possible negative consequences of acting. Bob was taking the route of apprehension that lead to being apprehensive.

• **Linda's Story**: Linda is CEO of a mid-market company. She has built a fine team that is producing at a very high level. Our sessions tended to be future focused. We talked about possibilities and probabilities. One of her strong points was the ability to grasp new and complex ideas and put them to work quickly. A second strength was an ability to see and understand what was going on around her and the people involved in the company.

Linda's approach to those people was different from Bob's. She spent a lot of time and effort working to understand what motivated them – but that understanding was seldom negative or limiting – and it never seemed to produce apprehension. She was driven by an essentially optimistic vision of the world and human potential. Challenge after challenge was met with the same optimism and determination. As a result, her team was very dedicated to the company and turnover was essentially zero.

But there is always a serpent in every Eden. For Linda, it was a tendency to overlook the negative and favor the positive estimates of every situation. As a result, the negatives were by and large ignored until they reached a crisis. When we boiled it all down, there was a similarity between Linda's and Bob's approach. His apprehension was driven by an appreciation of the risks that negatives brought to any situation. Her approach was driven by an aversion to thinking about the negatives.

• **Larry's Story**: Larry is a young entrepreneur who has never successfully built a business. But he keeps on trying – he is now on his fourth try. I was asked to advise Larry by the investors in his current company. They were concerned that expected results were not being achieved and that the company had settled into a pattern and culture that seemed to limit its future prospects.

My first session with Larry surfaced a major problem – a tendency that seemed at the root of much of his behavior. He had graduated from a top-of-the-line business school – earned both a bachelors and master's degree from the same program. As if often the case with young entrepreneurs, he was certain that he knew much more than he actually did. This hubris had a tendency to surface in 'gotcha' reactions. Larry was fond of manipulating conversations until he could 'spring the trap'. As are result, he ended up detonating relationships that might have proved important to the future of his company.

The company had gone through two almost complete turnovers of the senior team. Most had left quietly but two had made a bit of noise before departing. It was clear to me that, until Larry slaughtered his 'gotcha' daemon, nothing much positive would come out of the company.

I considered the situation so explosive that I scheduled a meeting with the investors. I outlined my findings. Two of the investors immediately agreed with me – they had had similar experiences with Larry. It was my recommendation that needed to be discussed carefully. As I saw it, there were only two options. The first was to confront Larry with his behavior and its effects on the business – and to stay with that confrontation until he changed. The second was to replace him as CEO. Neither were low-risk options. But the investors agreed that something had to be done – large amounts of capital were being frittered away while Larry played 'cop on the beat'.

Three Stories – One Root Cause: Although each of these stories sounds different, the root cause was the same. Each behavior was driven by an aversion that rested on an apprehension of the first type. Bob could not focus on anything but the negatives. Linda saw the positives because she could not bring herself to acknowledge the negatives. And Larry saw the whole world in a negative light – they were all criminals waiting to be exposed by the 'smart cop'. The idea of 'fearful expectation or anticipation' drove them all.

So What's That Got to do with Me? We all tell ourselves stories about whom and how we are. For the most part, these stories cast us in positive light. What that light hides in the shadows is the point. The 'of course, I am this way' story is a human constant. But it is never the whole story.

Maybe this will help. How often – some time later – have you realized something important about an event or something someone was trying to tell you? My record is about thirty years. It took me all that time and lots of experiences to finally realize what a friend was working hard to help me understand. My tragedy was that he had died before the light went on – I never got to thank him. But in my 'story' – probably like yours – I always have "a solid understanding of the situation and its implications".

Most of the time – and in spite of good intentions – we live out the first definition of apprehension. Every once in a while we manage to see a situation clearly and understand rather than fear its implications. With practice and dedication, we can improve that percentage. It is a matter of what the Buddhist call living in the present. Practice may not make perfect – but understanding is better than fear. For each of us, humanity hangs in the balance and, without that, we are just bumps in the road.

~~~~~~~~~

Your Life as a Work in Progress

One of the first steps in my mentoring engagements is to have the client begin to understand that their life is a work in progress. The deeper we get into it, the more detailed that understanding becomes. Then there is the recognition that life is a process which begins at birth and continues until death. But recognition is only the first step. It is an important one to be sure, but the best comes after that. We can begin to focus on the value of each of us and the positive impact that we can have on the lives of others.

Step One – Assessment

We begin with a self-assessment. Our objective is to develop a clearer understanding of the life which has emerged. Most of my clients begin this phase with some confidence that they understand the life they are living and how it came to be. But that certainty is replaced with a deeper understanding that overturns many of their cherished assumptions. In a fundamental way, they are meeting themselves for the first time. As casual assumptions are replaced by deeper self-knowledge, a far different picture begins to emerge.

One exercise that I use involves a self-description. I ask them to write one in as much detail as they can manage. For the most part, these paragraphs tend to be rather generic. They could be a description of most people. The hopes and dreams, strengths and faults, opportunities and limits are described in very general terms. It is a start, but only a start. Nothing much of that initial description survives the process as we begin to move from the generic to the specific. The driver for the process is a very simple set of questions.

- Tell me about yourself

- What kind of a person are you?
- What do you think are your strongest points?
- What are your weaknesses?
- How do people around you see you?
- What do you stand for?
- What do you tolerate?
- What about you makes you most proud?
- What about you gives you pause?

The first responses to these questions are an outline of the, almost casual, vision that each of us evolves during our life. Most answers are cast in positive value-loaded language. Nobody wants to see themselves as a negative person. But, using these initial responses as a baseline, we begin the journey of self-discovery. The results are almost always far more positive and empowering than the generic description. My clients begin to discover that they are much more complex and important than they assumed.

Step Two: Meeting Yourself

The assessment is a kind of snapshot; a picture frozen in time. Once we begin to fill out the details, the vision shifts to that work in progress. The idea of a person who is complete falls away and is replaced. Meeting yourself involves recognizing the things that are going on in your life and understanding why and how you are managing them. It means meeting yourself as a work in progress.

One you start to see yourself in this greater detail, your self-image becomes richer and more detailed. A sense of progress in some areas and lack of progress in others highlights important details of the life you have been living. Some of these efforts seem positive and empowering while others look limiting. The process of working forward from the baseline involves asking at each point, *'I know that I said that that this is the way I am, but am I really this way'?* It also means asking, *'I always thought that this is what I stand for. Is it really'?*

Step Three: Finding Good Mirrors

Early in the process, it is important to draw in other perspectives. Part of my mentoring involves building a support network of close friends. These serve as 'mirrors'; the better the friends, the better the mirrors. It is always important to have these sources to validate what you are telling yourself you are. We all need to understand the critical importance of these 'veracity checks'. An old friend and mentor was fond of saying, *"I've never met anyone who could tell it completely straight, including me"*. The truth is that each of us has become very good at misrepresenting ourselves in ways that even we cannot detect. The irony is that most of these misrepresentations distort rather than reflect our true nature.

So we develop a support structure to check our conclusions and, most of the time, the reflections tell us that we are selling ourselves short.

Step Four: Getting to Know Yourself

Once the assessment, initial introduction and support system are accomplished the really fun work begins. Most of my clients comment that many of their initial apprehensions tend to disappear. They have been avoiding getting to know themselves because of what the psychologists call 'a suspicion of self-bad-faith'. But they end up finding that they are really a much better, more interesting and important person than they ever allowed themselves to hope.

The initial work is hard and many times I have to push my clients to do the work. But once they are 'over the hump', I often have to run to keep up. One client recently told me, *"I had no idea that I was this interesting and positive a person. Why have I been avoiding myself for so long?"* She had finally met herself and liked what she saw. It was one of those 'and then the sun came up' moments.

Step Five: Becoming Who You Are

The core realization is that you are really a far better and more interesting person than you ever allowed yourself to suspect. The positive parts of your life can then be identified and magnified. The negative ones can be reduced and eventually eliminated. But all of that becomes possible only if you first become who you are and accept yourself as a wonderful person with tremendous potential. Everybody has parts of their life that they would rather not have known. And sure, we work on eliminating them. But the greatest part of our work is the discovery of those unique and positive parts that bring value to you and the people around you.

~~~~~~~~~~

__Finding a Mirror – Realizing__

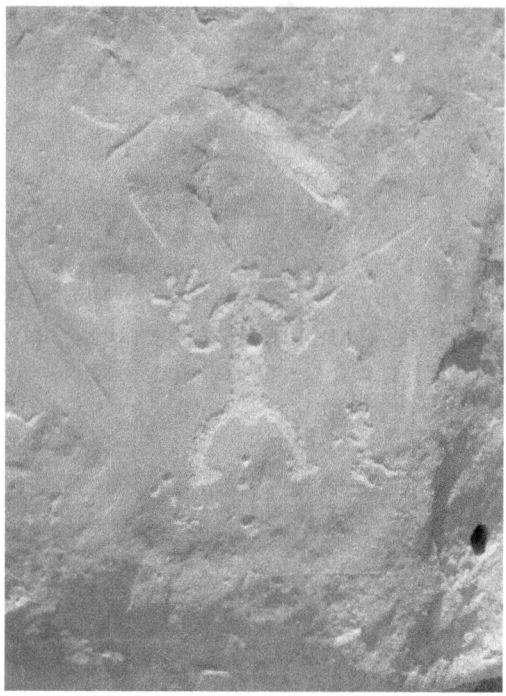

*We look in them every day – and use them as metaphors for
achieving deeper self-knowledge. Every person we meet is
one and what they show us can be far more valuable than
any highly polished surface.*

~~~~~~~~~~~~~~~~~~~~

I won't sugarcoat it – mentoring can bring some very
aggravating experiences. Sometimes it takes forever to
achieve just a small illumination. Then there are the times –
backsliding – when months of work seems to be washed
away by a recidivist tendency. But then there are the other
kinds that make the occasional frustration fade into the
background. Let me tell you about one of these experiences.

I was working with a senior team member – let's call him X – in a one-on-one mentoring engagement. This person is very bright and mentally agile – used to dealing with and developing creative solutions to very complex problems. He was an important asset to every team he was called to. However, there was a downside to his participation – he had a strongly anti-humanist attitude towards other people.

A couple of examples of this behavior might help you better understand why this was so great a problem.

His attitude toward lesser experienced team members was often dismissive. He came on as imperious – often taken by the victims of his behavior as hubris. More than once I had seen him 'cut the knees off' of a junior member of the team who was – albeit hesitatingly – advancing a possible solution to the challenge before the team. And more than once the solution that this 'underling' had suggested turned out to be the right path forward.

We talked about this tendency. But I quickly realized that for X this was an intellectual exercise – a logical inquiry into an area that was virtual and did not relate to either him or the 'real world'. Even when he was admitting that he behaved in such a manner, it was as if he was talking about someone else.

A second example – he tended to insist on exactly the same role in every team. His self-image was heavily colored by seeing himself as the 'idea generator' – the person who could see the way forward well before others did. This behavior fed into the first area. But it also created problems of its own. This was particularly true when solutions called for multidisciplinary contributions. In X's mind, there was only room for one 'creative guy' on any team.

The mentoring sessions had settled into a fairly repetitious pattern and I was getting ready to call the whole thing off – I have little appetite for kamikaze raids on vacant lots – when something most unexpected happened. As we began a session, I got the strong impression that something had happened – something that X really wanted to talk about but was having difficulty finding the right place to start. I figured that a bit of distraction would help him so I asked "how was your weekend?"

"That's what I wanted to talk to you about", came the reply. "Something happened that made me realize something about myself."

I wasn't sure what to make of this. All of our conversations had been about work related issues. I expected to hear about some family issue or argument. But that was not what X wanted to talk about.

"I had decided to take a drive out to the mountains – just to get away for an afternoon and relax", he said. "I was going to a place that I really like to hike through. I left the main road and drove along a narrow one that eventually turned into a dirt road. About a mile into that road, I had a flat tire."

I wasn't sure where this was going but X really needed to tell me about it – so I went along for the ride.

"When I got to the trunk, I found the jack, spare tire but no lug wrench. It was then that I remembered that I had taken it out of the trunk and forgot to put it back. So I had to walk along the road until I came to a farm. It took me a while to find the farmer – a nice guy – who listened to my dilemma – went into the barn – and came out with one of those four-way lug wrenches. We walked back to my car and the farmer proceeded to jack the car up and replace the flat tire with the spare."

At this point, X hesitated – I knew we were coming to the 'crunchy' part of the story.

"Well, to make a long story short, I kept on telling this guy that he was going about it all wrong. I thought that I was trying to help him get it right. But that is not how it worked out. After a couple of comments, the farmer stood up and said, "I have work to do and my cows are pleasanter company". At that, he walked down the road towards his farm."

"So", I asked, "you met your enemy and you are he?"

He looked at me sheepishly and smiled. "Yeah, that's what occurred to me." As I stood there in the middle of this dirt road with the person who had the tools and knowledge to solve my problem heading away, I said to myself 'OK, wise ass – nice job – now what?' But then all of those times I had acted just like the farmer had came flooding back.

To say it was confusing is an understatement. So I sat down on a rock at the side of the road to think about what had just happened. I was sitting there about half an hour when the farmer came back. Without saying a work, he set to changing the tire. When he finally finished and had put the tools and flat tire back into the trunk, he turned to me and said, "even dumb animals deserve our help – yeah, particularly dumb animals." Then he walked back towards his farm.

"I stood there for a minute or two absolutely speechless and then broke out in a loud belly-laugh. At hearing me, the farmer turned half-way towards me, flashed a big smile, waved and continued back to his farm."

Epiphanies come in the strangest wrappers sometimes. A couple of hours on a dirt road had accomplished more than a dozen mentoring sessions.

~~~~~~~~~~

Getting the Right Personal Vision

Lots of advice is available. The common mantra is 'get a personal vision'. But the truth is that you already have one. Sure, it may be out of focus and counterproductive. But you do have one. Many would call it your 'self-image'. It is how you decide what you will do and what you will not do. This self-image sets your expectations. It holds your private vision of you in the world. It is there with you when you wake up every morning and as you go to sleep each night. So, the question is not whether you have a personal vision. The question is 'do you have the right personal vision?"

All personal visions are compelling. They control your life and expectations. Your personal vision gets you out of bed every morning and moves you through the day. At the end of each day you have experienced the meaning of your vision. Each of your days is guided by it. So, if at the end of a day you are dissatisfied with the way it went, you need to look to your personal vision and ask 'am I journeying through life with the wrong one?"

The right personal vision moves you in the direction your life should take rather than one chosen by chance. It gives you a clear understanding of who you are, what you are entitled to and what contributions you can make to the world as you find it. The right personal vision gives you confidence that you are valuable in your own right, that you are entitled to be treated with respect and consideration and that you can make important contributions to the lives of people around you.

You can make changes in your life and those changes are best begun with a search for the right personal vision. My mentoring work begins with this search. It is not as hard as you might think. You need to start with the support of a guide and make the commitment to keep on until you have reached that self-understanding that will reveal the personal vision that is uniquely for you.

Overcoming the Internal Arguments

So what stands in your way? The first is your own inertia. Once you have made an accommodation with life and settled for a personal vision that is a poor fit, you turn that vision into a series of habits. You might consistently underestimate your value to other people, for instance. Once that becomes a habit and part of your personal vision, it is very hard to change the underlying behavior. In a strange way, it involves arguing with yourself.

- You: You need to stop being that way

- *You: This is the way I am*

- You: Being this way is harming my life and limiting its potential

- *You: This is the way I am*

- You: I need to change, to become the personal I can be not the one I became

- *You: I do not like change*

- You: I will change and find a better personal vision

- *You: I will fight you on this. This means war!*

Once you decide to search for a better personal vision, these kinds of internal discussions are unavoidable. It is not that you like your current vision. You might be either ashamed or uncertain about your place and role in the world. Maybe there is a small voice that keeps suggesting a change. But that voice is drowned out by the insistence of the current vision of you.

Step One: Gather the Courage to Listen to That Small Voice

The first step is by far the most difficult. It takes a great deal of courage to contradict yourself; and that is exactly what you have to do. Part of you will insist that things are manageable if not optimal. Change is dangerous and involves the unknown. The push-back can be daunting. But you must not be daunted. The way forward is through that resistance. There is no way around it. You must push through it.

One way to overcome your own resistance is to build a support network around your project of self-reinvention. One mistake people make is to keep their resolve to themselves and not share it with others. Behavior change is hard enough with the help of your friends. You do not want to be locked alone in a dark room with your own aversion to change. Declare your intentions to those around you and ask their help in monitoring your progress. You will receive two gifts if you do this. The first is the support of your friends. The second is the gift that you will give them. Beyond a statement of faith in their friendship, you will also give them an example of what they might achieve if they decided to try.

Chart your course and then set about following it. Begin by writing out a clear statement of intention. Make sure that you keep that statement focused on your daily life. Remember, you are setting out on a search for a better personal vision. The constant questions should be:

- Who am I and what excites me about living?
- What do I bring to the world that is uniquely mine?
- What can I invest my time in that will give me the greatest return?

- What returns do I value the most?

The answers to these questions are as unique for you as they are for every other person. The more work you put into developing the answers, the more unique they become. You see, a personal vision should be, first and foremost, personal. It should relate directly to the world as you find it and to the people around you. Here is an Example of what I mean:

- Who am I and what excites me about living?
- *I enjoy spending time with X. He brings me new ideas and possibilities*
- What do I bring to the world that is uniquely mine?
- *I seem to be able to see the possibilities that X brings and turn them into actions*
- What can I invest my time in that will give me the greatest return?
- *I need to spend more time with X and turning his ideas into actions*
- What returns do I value the most?
- *The biggest payoff for working with X is the joy I get from helping others along their journey*

If you spend some time thinking this way, you will quickly discover many 'starting points'. Maybe you have just not focused on those things in your life that do excite you. But they are there for you to find. Remember to keep your focus on your daily life. Do not get caught up in 'strategic think'. Each series of answers should relate to something that you actually can do in the day you are living through.

Step Two: Make it a Journey

Realization is an interesting word. It has two meanings. The first is to realize something. That meaning relates to the idea of understanding. For example, 'I realized that I was standing too close to the edge of the Grand Canyon'. There is that 'ah ha' moment of realization. The second meaning relates to accomplishment. 'At my graduation, I realized a life goal of completing a university education'. So you see that realizing that you need to find a better personal vision is only the first step along the path to realizing the goal of having it.

Like most journeys, the search for a new personal vision is full of stop, go, forward, back sliding and many ups and downs. For instance, you do not work on it twenty-four hours a day. In the time between, you have the opportunity to realize the goals you have set for yourself. Some you will make and celebrate the success. Others you will miss and vow to try again.

A good rule of thumb is that it takes about two months to make a new habit and about twice that to overcome an entrenched one. It is important to see your efforts as a journey that you have committed to. You need to become and remain disciplined and focused. It is important that you see the journey in terms of progress and movement. Remember, you are working to overcome the inertia that kept you stuck in an unproductive personal vision. A good vision of the process will involve a journey from the stifling atmosphere of a confining rut to the clear and invigorating air of a open meadow on a sunny day. The more you are able to see your efforts in this light, the better your chances of continuing on the journey and realizing your goal.

Each step of the journey should be seen as a chance to experience your personal development towards a better place. It is your journey and your place that you are going to. That meadow is your meadow and only yours. It is the place of all places in the world that you ought to be. Moving towards it means finding and following your true north. That is the direction that you life should take to lead you to that place.

Step Three: Accounting for Yourself

This journey you are on has its own kind of accounting. Each action has a cost and benefit. Some the costs are incurred because you want to get somewhere. For instance, you may spend time reading about an idea or learning a new skill. You make the investment to be able to understand better or make bigger contributions to the people around you. Other costs come because you are operating with the wrong personal vision. You have the costs of lost time or opportunity but no balancing gain to show for it.

Some returns, once they are achieved, do not seem to have the expected value. How often have you responded out of anger towards a situation or person only to realize later that you should have held your temper and moved towards the mutual benefit that was there for both of you? Why did you settle for the bogus return of anger when the gem of mutual benefit was there to be shared? Another example might be those people who dedicate their lives to scrambling after celebrity. Many of them will do almost anything to be famous; if for only fifteen minutes. But the graveyard of their lives is the final realization that nothing of value was being pursued.

Then there are the returns which are so valuable that they need to be cherished and honored. Each step you make towards your own true personal vision is such a return. Each goal you realize is another. Every time you make an effort and drive through the resistance, you give yourself a gift of rare value.

Step Four: Celebrate Your Victories and Redouble Efforts to Overturn Your Defeats

Remember to honor your dedication to this journey. You will stay motivated as long as you reinforce your resolve by celebrating your successes along the way. As you move forward, your vision will become so compelling and empowering that you will do anything to achieve it. Once you reach that level of commitment, nothing will keep you from the goals you have set. Your quest of the right personal vision will be there in the morning when you awake and with you all through the day. It will be with you as you fall asleep and inhabit your dreams. Your quest will become the core of whom you are and who you can become. It will define your mark on the world and contribution to the people around you. It will define you as a unique and important person who is in touch with your value and ability to contribute. It will make your life your own.

~~~~~~~~~~

Reason Why or Thinking How?

Some of my mentoring engagements focus on the personal tendencies of my clients. Those journeys take us into very personal areas; many of which have been either avoided or ignored for many years. One of the most productive assaults centers around a tendency that is ubiquitous among humans – enabled by the human capacity for selective memory.

Explanations instead of solutions: There are many self-help gurus who insist that the secret to present behavior is to be found in your past experiences – 'the past is prologue'. Most forms of analysis fare centered on this idea. The theory is that, if you can come to terms with why you are doing something – behaving in certain self-destructive or self-limiting ways – you will be able to change those behaviors. There is a fundamental flaw here. If it was true then historians would be making current history as they analyze the past. But they aren't.

The problem is that analysis tends to generate explanations rather than solutions. You may end up knowing 'why' you are behaving in a self-destructive way and find that, having the explanation, you are not able to make the changes necessary to stop the behavior.

~~~~~~

This is an important and very subtle point that merits careful reflection. All self-destructive or self-limiting behaviors interpenetrate attempts to analyze them. Following the observation 'no matter where you go, there you are', the tendency to be this way or that cannot be left behind when thinking about the tendency to be this way or that.

~~~~~~

The Simplistic Holistic: Another weakness of analysis of the past as a foundation for changing the future is that it tends to focus too broadly. It ignores the ancient wisdom – a journey of a thousand miles begins with a single step. In fact, too much reflection on the past can result in analysis paralysis. Life becomes like those nightmares that we all experience at least once – of being rooted in a spot and dreading the approach of some calamity. Many forms of analysis only serve to increase the dread. They give you no guidance that can be translated into effective action.

'How' Not 'Why': You see, the question that you need to ask begins with 'how' rather than 'why'. I remember working with a client a few years back. Sam was a very successful, well-educated and literate senior executive. He had a tendency to self-sabotage that was very frustrating. Sam had built, or participated in the building of, several companies. He was widely recognized as someone who could 'pull it together and make it work'. But, sooner or later, his tendencies began to destabilize the companies.

As our sessions began, it was clear that Sam had a very good grasp of the history and impact of his behaviors. He could talk for hours about how he behaved and why he thought that he behaved that way. But it quickly became clear that he had no idea about how to stop behaving that way. He was an expert on 'why' he behaved as he did but could not answer the question 'how' do I behave differently.

The Simplistic Holistic Revisited: As we worked through our sessions, I began to challenge Sam to come up with ideas – ways that he could change his behavior. At first, the conversations tended to return to the analysis. The habit of substituting reflection for action was strongly rooted in his personality. But we persisted. Things got so hot a number of times that I was almost fired as his coach. Once he actually fired me. But he learned that I was more dedicated to his success than he was and, slightly embarrassed at the time, he returned to the engagement.

Finally we began to overcome Sam's tendency to address the whole problem all at once. We were able to identify a few small steps that would take him off the path he had been on and begin to forge a new one. It was frustrating for Sam because he wanted to see the connection all the way from where he was to where he was going. But he finally hunkered down and began to make the changes.

Direction? What Direction? Once Sam let go of the holistic tendency, we were able to begin to change his behavior. He was still bothered by the lack of a 'strategic plan' for the process. But he soldered on. My mantra in those days was 'any movement is better than none – any direction is the right one as long as it is away from where you are.'

Sam had learned an important lesson along the way. He stopped thinking about 'why' he did things and started thinking about 'how' he could improve results. By that single act – moving from 'why' to 'how' – Sam took the first step in renovating his life and remaking his future. It wasn't an easy thing and I credit him for the courage it took. The journey continues for him – as does our work together – but now it is a different thing. Now we work on making the future rather than selectively editing and interpreting the past.

~~~~~~~~~~

Fighting the Wrong Battles

Mentoring is a profession easy to get into and very hard to master. I am often taken aback by the lack of experience that some 'mentors' have. They seem to have fallen into the profession by default. One 'coach' told me that she became a coach because she "couldn't think of anything else to do." Another had a series of failures in his attempt to start businesses and thought it would be easier to "help others with theirs". Strangely, this syndrome is akin to a challenge that some of my mentoring clients face. Let me tell you a story that might help you understand.

~~~~~~

It seems a cop was walking his beat one evening when he came across a man on his hands and knees under one of the corner streetlamps. He watched the man crawl back and forth on the sidewalk for a while and, eventually, his curiosity got the better of him. He asked the man "did you lose something?"

"Yes", the man replied. "I've lost my wallet. It's got all my money, credit cards and identification in it."

The cop offered to help the man find his wallet and asked, "where were you when you noticed that the wallet was missing?"

The man pointed back along the block and said, "about half way to the corner."

The cop had a bit of trouble with the response and asked the obvious question. "If you lost your wallet back there in the middle of the block, why are you looking for it here?"

The man looked up at the cop in disbelief. "The light's better here", he replied.

The tendency to fight the battles you are comfortable with rather than the ones you need to win is a normal human tendency. I once worked with a client who struggled with his weight. He spent a lot of time thinking, worrying, reading and consulting doctors, consultants and all manner of experts. As we worked together it became clear that 'battle' was a distraction from the real challenge before him. He had started a company and labored under the burden of suspecting that he was not up to it. His losing battle with his waistline was taken as reinforcement of that suspicion.

Two Roads ...: The first series of sessions were rough on us both. But I had the experience of walking through the inevitable fire before. A less experienced coach might take the issue of self-control as the central one – and would fail in their efforts. There are times when the past and looking back gets in the way.

His focus on controlling his weight was a diversion and reflected an addiction to 'self-reflection' and 'self-mortification'. The single most damaging effect of 'past-oriented- thinking is that it generates excuses rather than solutions. Here the excuse was a complex mesh of wrong-focus and self-sabotaging failures. The client was safe from having to deal with the central challenge as long as the faux one was front and center. Failure in dealing with the faux challenge insulated him from having to come to terms with the central challenge. The pact was with his own devils and he was jailer and prisoner all in one.

It was tough getting him to give up the focus on his weight. There was tenseness in our early sessions that made it very difficult to see any progress. But I kept returning to the same course. "Forget about why you can't seem to lose weight – how are we going to build your business and harvest the value you have created."

I got 'fired' three or four times – nothing new for me – and several of our sessions ended up with heated words. But my experience was telling me that if he could find the courage to deal with the central challenge, the rest would take care of itself. Things came to a head when, in frustration, he said, "ok, it's not working my way – let's try it yours'.

We began with small steps – teeny, as truth be told. But we kept at it and made one change after another in how he was approaching his business. It took a couple of months or reinforcement for the new behaviors to become new habits but, to his credit, he kept at it. But there was something else – something that I hesitated to mention to him because I thought it might trigger a bit of backsliding.

Then he brought it up. "You know that for the first time in ten years, I have been losing weight?"

"Oh really, I hadn't noticed," I offered with a grin.

~~~~~~~~~~~

Finding the Right Battles

In Fighting the Wrong Battles I suggested that much time and energy was wasted in fighting the wrong battles. That article generated quite a few responses. They varied from agreement through incredulity to outright disagreement. I suggested that most of the 'battles' that we wage are really straw men – distractions from the challenges that we ought to face.

I wanted to deal with a couple of the most interesting responses as they highlight reasons why individuals don't manage to change course and end up sailing in the tight small circle.

One individual objected to my characterization of weight loss efforts as a distraction. He suggested that it was a laudable goal to reach a 'healthy weight'. Certainly, in today's world, it is easy to find people who would agree with him. I see them all the time when I take my daily trips around the track next door. In fact, there is a whole industry out there which constantly assaults us with the next best thing that will put you on the road to that healthy nirvana. But then I wonder. I recently heard someone observe that becoming a healthy office rat is not much of an improvement. The 'office rat' designation was the one that was important. They were talking about the life balance between work and self.

This fellow seems to have a good point. What is the use of being healthy if your healthy life is the surface manifestation of an unhealthy existence? Putting aside the argument over what is healthy and the one-size-fits-all contentions of these weight gurus, it seems to me that the individual needs to ask the questions "is this the battle I really need to fight? If I win it, will my life be that much better than it is now?"

Now I am not advocating that we all let ourselves go and become obese. I am suggesting that spending time and money on that battle may not make out lives very much better. It is, after all, easily possible to be fit and live a life or quiet desperation.

Another response took a different line. This person wrote that she was stuck in a job that she couldn't stand and saw no options. I hear this a lot. The battle against a job that you can't stand is not nearly as important as the battle to find one that you love. Go back and re-read the article – particularly the part about the man and the streetlight. Isn't that exactly the way this person was fighting her battle? She was in a job – that was where the light was – and that was the battle she chose to fight. As a result, the real battle – the one that would set her on a course to a brighter future – was being foregone.

The very difficult problem in finding the right battles to fight is that we are so good at deluding ourselves – so very good that our chances of overcoming avoidance tendencies and finding the right ones is very slim if we attempt the search on our own. At the core of this dilemma is a tendency towards self-sabotaging behaviors. One of the great benefits of working with an experienced coach is that they have trod these roads before and know the kinds of tricks we play on ourselves.

Call it mentoring – or, if it is easier, call it mentoring. The distinction isn't as important as understanding the dynamics of the relationship. People who have made contributions to my life have done so by calling me out when I mistake dalliance for progress – mistake the swamp for solid ground – the mist for clarity – and myself as my own best friend. The road forward is difficult enough. Fighting the wrong battles only makes it more difficult and frustrating. Finding the right ones to wage means breaking through those delusions and into the clear, fresh and unpolluted air that sustains growth.

~~~~~~~~~~

To 'E' or to 'O'?

Most of my early-stage advisory engagements initially focus on helping the 'CEO' understand what it means to be a CEO. That understanding – or lack thereof – can have a determining impact on a company's future.

~~~~~~~~~~~~~~~~~~~~

Within the dim and fading mists of the history of every start-up lies the seed of its own destruction ... or at least of its own stunted growth. As errors go, this 'myth of fingerprints' is one of the most frequent misunderstandings of what a growing company needs and what will happen if it does not get what it needs.

Let's start with a general description. A founder and a few small team members are running a company. They are successful in getting the thing off the ground by hard work and very long hours. The team's dedication and persistence is paying off ... the company is growing. The Founder adopts the title CEO (sometimes CEO and President, which I have always found a bit much or, worse yet, Chairman and CEO) and becomes the 'Chief of Everything'. The rest of the team are similarly blessed with high sounding titles right out of larger corporate culture. The chief recruiter is given the title Vice President of Human Resources. The controller becomes the Chief Financial Officer. There may even be a CIO or CTO in a company running less than $5,000,000 in annual revenue. Quite often there is no Chief Operating Officer (COO). I have never encountered a team with a Chief Administrative Officer ... even the title CAO.

So what's the problem Chief? Well, there are two. The first, and a subject of a later column, is that people get titles far beyond their experiences, capabilities and competencies ... and that creates real problems later on. The second, and my focus here, is that the job description for the CEO as 'Chief of Everything' becomes inherently limiting of the company's future. Here is a way that you, CEO, might understand what I am getting at. Let's take a quick trip into the realm of complexity theory for a fresh, and possibly liberating, view of the landscape.

Find some quiet time for reflection ... sit down in your most comfortable chair ... clear your mind of the day-to-day minutia ... then try to see your Company as a complex self-organizing system ... a living thing with its own needs independent of yours ... in other words your 'child'. Then introduce the idea that 'organizations evolve more quickly than the people in them'. Your child is evolving more quickly than you, as its parent, are capable of changing to meet its needs.

Here are some of the problems that your child might be having with you.

- The Personality Cult and its corrosive effects ... if it's all about you then ...

- The Peter Pan Syndrome ... if you won't grow up then ...

The Napoleonic Complex ... if it is all about your vision then ...

There are good reasons why the CEO has evolved into the Chief Business Development Officer in successful privately owned companies. Very good reasons why that person has to distance themselves from the day to day operations ... delegating those responsibilities to first a COO and then a CAO. And this means that a CEO has to decide to be a CEO and stop being a COO. If a CEO does not see or accept these reasons, most often the effect is to limit the growth of the company ... for filling these needs is central to that growth and the CEO is the only one to do it.

148

The CEO has to manage the evolution of the team ... make the hard decisions. For example, some of the people who got you to the early successes are not those who will help you take the Company to a sixty or one hundred million dollar run rate.

In short, a CEO has to put personal evolution on the fast track ... and get that evolution mostly right ... in order to help the Company to realize its potential. But how do you learn what you have never directly experienced? How does a CEO gather the wisdom? The solution is as hard to manage as it is simple to state. You get yourself a network of mentors ... individuals who have climbed the mountain you are seeking to conquer. But how? Here is one recipe that I have seen work well.

- First find an individual with a long track record of success and develop a close personal relationship

- Make sure that the track record includes multiple successes in the CEO role. In other words, avoid the 'they that can't do teach' trap

- Engage that person in a highly formal way ... introduce them into your corporate culture

- Ask that person to assemble an Advisory Board of mentors in various areas ... sales, marketing, operations, etc.

- Then use the combined wisdom and experience of the Board as both a guide and accelerator of your own development.

Two pieces of advice here. First, don't try to build the Board yourself. If you do, you will most likely take the easy way out and build a 'soft' Board that will not challenge you. Second, clear the time to interact with and learn from the Board members. It will take far more time that you initially think. To have an Advisory Board is not the same as benefiting from one. I have seen many that essentially do nothing and are paid for it.

The lesson here is clear. A CEO must run to keep up with the evolving needs of the Company. Failure means that your child will end up digging ditches instead of moving mountains.

~~~~~~~~~~

OK ... its 'O' Now What?

Once a founder begins to come to terms with what it means to be a CEO, there are choices to be made. The first is, what will be their role in the company as it grows. The answer is not foregone and a real test of the founder's maturity and willingness to subordinate their ego to the needs of the company.

~~~~~~~~~~~~~~~~~~~~

Several years back I wrote a monthly column for a national sheep magazine. (Yes, there was and still is such a thing!) I dealt with a range of subjects surrounding modern flock management. One of my columns focused on the habit of some shepherds with flocks under five hundred head to make their own hay ... instead of buying it at auction. As I remember I termed the practice 'stump dumb'.

One of my readers had settled down in his easy chair on a winter's night to read the column. As he told my editors later, he got so mad at me that he flung the magazine across the room and swore never to read it again.

But something changed his mind. About a month later he was out in the barn getting the equipment ready for the planting, tending and harvesting seasons. He said' "I stopped dead and looked around at the investment I had tied up in all that equipment ... drills, tedders, tractors, bailers, wagons and such ... and I said to myself 'well, I'll be damned! That Jackass is right. This is stump dumb.'

So, maybe you have read my last column and had a similar reaction. Hopefully you have made the entire journey. I hope so ... because, if you haven't, this column is going to be a hard slog.

Let's assume that you have recognized the need to be a true CEO in your start-up team. You have decided not to be the chief limiting factor in your companies' potential for growth. Now what? Well, here is the first 'what' that you should consider … and it is a trap that many new CEOs fall into. Should you be the lead business development representative of your company or its lead fundraiser?

Now make me proud and think about this one a bit.

Here is the trap … and I have seen it more times that I can count. The CEO takes on the task of raising venture capital. As the tallest hog at the trough, he siphons off the time and energies of the best and brightest within his team … and the rest are left to actually build the business. This is a recipe for failure … and I have seen many a CEO run down that path until it petered out into oblivion.

The CEO of a start-up should be dedicated to building a customer base for the business … period, paragraph. All of his energies should center on this priority. It is not the technology that is important … it is the fact that there are customers whose checks regularly clear and who are willing to pay for the technology that is important. A viable business is defined by its customers not its venture investors

"But how are we to grow without getting the financial resources we need?", comes the clarion cry. Well, and this is going to come as a real shock to some, the 'need' for financial resources may be less of a 'given' in your case than an indicator that you are neither very good or particularly suited for growing a business from the CEO seat. Additionally, there may be other, much less expensive ways to provide those resources.

Many a large company has been built without venture capital on a happy and expanding customer base … none that I know of have managed the reverse.

Venture capitalists are a lot like bankers. If you have what they want they will find you and break down the doors trying to get at it. If you don't, you won't get much beyond a smile and the cup of coffee that came during your presentation. But if you have gathered that I am suggesting that the CEO should not be the lead in seeking venture funding, the question naturally comes "Well, who should lead the charge and what should the value proposition be?" OK, let's try a little role playing.

You are a partner in Rub-A-Dub Ventures. You have just said goodbye to yet another eager young team of 'entrepreneurs' with a PowerPoint presentation, business plan and not a real customer in sight. Your headache had been getting worse as the day wears on. But your next meeting is different. In come a couple of senior executives … happy customers of a company that they want to talk to you about investing in. This company is managed by a team that has not only made them happy … but has made a growing client base happy as well. The CEO of this company is so dedicated to customer satisfaction that he has had to skip this meeting to discuss a new business initiative with a client.

OK Mr. Rub-A-Dub, what do you do? If you have any sense at all, you tell your assistant to cancel your appointments for the rest of the day … you have just found your next deal.

This scenario … in one variation or another … happens all of the time. I know partners in private equity funds that have made fortunes by talking to customers first. Here is their rule … and it should be yours. Smart venture capitalists don't invest in technologies they invest in teams that can implement their marketing plans. And you can identify such a team by three principal characteristics. First, they have customers rather than markets. Second, they have a run rate rather than a burn rate. And third, the CEO is leading the charge to build the customer base.

~~~~~~~~~~

153

The 'Completeness Doctrine'

A while back I was having drinks with a friend who has been involved in mentoring senior executives for several decades. During the course of that conversation he offered an interesting and challenging question: "Why is it that some executives find it so difficult to change behaviors in the face of overwhelming evidence that 1) the behaviors are counterproductive at best and often destructive and 2) that such changes will probably radically improve their effectiveness as a leader ... and their contributions to their company?"

When asked what the source of the question was, he

recounted a series of mentoring situations with much the same (and clearly to him highly frustrating) outcomes. In each case a CEO had, after extended experience with the limiting destructiveness of their own personal tendencies, come up against the distinct possibility that their behavior, rather than the world at large, was the primary source of the factors which were stunting their company's growth.

As he went through the "case studies", the pattern quickly became clear. Philosophically the question became: "If humans are capable of rational thought then why doesn't rational thought trump counterproductive behavior in these kinds of situations?"

I responded initially with one of my favorite aphorisms: "*You can lead a horticulture, but you can't make her think!*" After a good laugh we decided that maybe that was as good a door as any through which to enter this darkened room.

My first foray began with the idea that, for some people, habits, particularly when they relate to important and closely held components of self-image and personality, are very hard to break. My idea was a variation of the old Chinese proverb that once a sheet of paper is folded it will always tend to re-fold in exactly the same place. I suggested that some behavior changes present more of a challenge because they require fundamental modifications in an individual's understanding of who they are. Under the theory that a person's self-image is accumulated over time and plays an essential part not only in defining who that person is to themselves but also what their appropriate place and status in the world is, I suggested that these CEOs were most likely to resist changing behaviors that have come to represent a central part of how they define themselves and how they prefer to be accepted by the world.

This suggestion took us down a path that meandered through a couple of drinks, some tasty, if somewhat overly spicy, hors d'oeuvres and about a half an hour of lively conversation. But the analysis, though logically satisfying, didn't seem to bring us much closer to an answer that might be useful. As satisfying as it was to come to the conclusion that, in some ways and in some situations, people are just stubbornly mulish, it didn't do much for two people who spend a lot of time and energy trying to help the mule get up and actually pull the wagon.

And, if we were going to attack the problem from that direction both of us should probably take a decade off and get an advanced degree in psychiatry! So I started to look for another possibility.

What was it about these CEOs that seemed to set them apart from others who didn't had the same problems with change? The question seemed daunting. They were a rather incoherent group ... managing companies across a range of sizes, industries and value propositions. Some had decades of experience while others were just starting out. There was no apparent dominant gender, age, ethnicity or race trait in the group. So what made them a group? And what caused them to have trouble with achieving fundamental change?

Sometime after the second drink I made a suggestion that seemed to promise a way up. "Maybe what is important is not the habits that are hard to break but that portion of a person's self-image that tells them they are either still on the journey or that they have arrived." Maybe this group is a group because all of them subscribe to what I call the "Completeness Doctrine".

I have been fond of observing that "organizations evolve much more quickly than the people who inhabit them". The idea here became "maybe these people have stopped learning. Perhaps they see themselves as fully formed ... arrived rather than on the journey. Maybe these people have stopped growing!"

We focused on the personalities of these CEOs and began to dig out some common characteristics. They all had been pretty much rounding the same small circles for years. As another friend is fond of saying, maybe "they get to confront the same problem over and over until they solve it and then get to go on to the next one." But, since they aren't capable of solving it, the circular journey continues and the behavior endures.

I left the conversation convinced that we had stumbled on something quite important. Acceptance of the "Completeness Doctrine" as part of an individual's self-image might create limits to growth and change merely through its acceptance. By such an acceptance, an individual might immediately create a whole family of challenges they will not be able to overcome simply because they closed the books before they developed the necessary skills … they have stopped learning before they have learned what is necessary to know.

On the drive home I remembered people that I had met while on Wall Street who, even well into their 80s, seemed reflexively to take the "student" role when facing the world or new challenges. The combination of wonder and curiosity that they carried with them in all their "adventures" seemed to re-arrive to my present musings and smile at me over the years … out of a remembrance that had been refreshed.

I have always thought of people who have stopped learning as a kind of "walking dead". Their recourse seemed to be to the pettier aspects of life, instrumental interpretations of reality and the delusions that seem to be so necessary to maintain a self-image that awaits only the grave. But now I found myself considering the costs … the terrible costs … that the living are often called upon to pay on account of these "fossils-of-the-once-alive".

I'm not sure what the usefulness of these thoughts is … particularly since I have little idea as to how one would go about re-starting the feelings of wonder and curiosity in an individual who has discarded them as distractions. Maybe their only use is a quarantine sign indicating "no-go" zones for the still living. Maybe the only usefulness of the "Completeness Doctrine" is as a kind of "scarlet letter" that should warn investors and potential followers to stay clear of the leper colony.

Or maybe Mary Shelley was right ... inorganic matter can be re-enlivened. Now that would be something to see and a cure for many a malaise.

Personally, I am on the side of the monster here. What has been done ill-considered must be capable of being undone with knowledge and will. Otherwise, why bother?

These 'leaders-in-the-swamps-and-mists' must be able to be brought out into the clear air and sunshine. Like all major surgery, it takes the removal of the diseased and the restoration of healthy ways of being.

~~~~~~~~~~

The Benefits of Knowing – The Costs of Not Knowing

An old friend used to say, "you never know how you look until you get your picture took". Taking the time to get an outside assessment can often save a company from charging down paths that lead either nowhere or to the edge of a cliff. The cost of not knowing can be higher than you ever imagined.

~~~~~~~~~~~~~~~~~~~~~

Strategic planning is very hard work ... which is why only companies that commit to a rigorous program benefit from it. A well-organized planning process begins with a focused assessment. Done correctly, this process can identify high impact areas where a company is delivering low performance. If not identified and corrected, low performance can quickly bleed away a company's future.

Self-assessment is a particularly difficult process. An individual may go years without recognizing those parts of their leadership style that are limiting their effectiveness and potential. CEOs and other rising stars can quickly turn into shooting stars without systematic help. Many companies are using modern leadership assessment tools to help their best hopes for the future identify and overcome limitations in their leadership style.

In both of these areas, effective web-enabled assessment tools are available for, and are being used worldwide by, companies that need a fast, reliable process to identify critical issues, re-align priorities and resourcing, and devise and implement effective strategic plans. Variations of these tools are also being used to assess corporate boards.

Today these tools take advantage of technology and extensive business research to provide management the reliable information needed to effectively focus on high-value activities. Many of these tools are web-enabled, minimally intrusive and based on solid research which relates results to best practices. They not only provide accurate diagnostics but help senior management to develop effective strategic plans for dealing with their organization's shortcomings.

Most of these tools identify high impact areas where a company is delivering low performance. They also can highlight areas of low impact where a company is spending excessively. Most start with the assumption that, beyond a certain stage in growth, a company's organization and operations are much more complicated than a human mind can think about intuitively. From my own experience I can tell you that many strategies have come out of these assessments which were both counter intuitive and highly effective.

These high impact tools, and their effective use, represent one of the most cost effective expenditures that a senior management team can make. Very few programs can give you the bang for the buck that you get from a well-focused assessment. And very few can go nearly as far in opening up the potential of your company, its leaders and its management team.

MAPs, LAPs, BAPs and GAPs: I have taken to referring to the assessment tools which I use as Web-Enabled Assessment Programs or WEAPs. I like that acronym because it reminds me of the cold water, wake-up call, slap in the face that a well-focused assessment can often produce. This is often followed by the inevitable question ... "How could I have gotten it that wrong?" Then enters the weeping. Assessment programs are not for sissies ... but the truth will set you free!

Assessment programs come in four flavors: Management

Assessment (MAP), Leadership Assessment (LAP), Board Assessment (BAP) and Global Assessment (GAP).

A MAP will allow you to quickly pin point your company's weaknesses and best opportunities for strategic improvement. It provides a solidly-based, fast track ability to identify, and agree on, those areas that are critical to your company's success … where your current performance compromises your company's ability to achieve that success.

With a LAP you can identify the attributes that will help you become a more effective leader. This kind of assessment is particularly useful to CEOs as it covers both leadership competence and character and draws data from several levels of the organization. It can help you reach an understanding of how your leadership style can be improved … how you can become more effective in your role.

A BAP focuses on a company's boards and areas such as strategic business development, succession planning, governance, oversight and compliance. It is a 'best practices' assessment that is completed by board members and senior management. Whether it is Sarbanes-Oxley, or other board related imperatives, this assessment supports the needs of organizations that are committed to board effectiveness.

A GAP will give you a holistic picture of your company, its leadership and board effectiveness. It produces a 360 by 360 assessment which can serve as the basis of a strategic plan or tactical review. It is by far the most powerful of the four as a GAP collects the same date as the other three combined but allows an integrated analysis and broader based understanding of the situation and possibilities.

Low Costs – High Impact: One thing that I learned early on was how cost effective an assessment process was. For a very modest investment you can get an organizational assessment done that will give you a solid idea where your company is falling short and how to correct it. Leadership style assessment and board assessment are the same. Incredibly inexpensive compared with the value received.

Cinderella is a fairy tale and business should not be seen as rolling the dice hoping that the glass slippers will turn up and fit. Business is a matter of tilting the table in your favor with superior preparation and stronger implementation.

A company can invest these very modest amounts and get results that will set it above its competition … or forgo those investments and lose out to a company that has made them. As elsewhere, here it is better to know than not know. As they say in the Marines, assumption is the mother of all foul-ups … or something like that.

A truth or two about knowing and not knowing: The costs of under-performance and misalignment are just as real as any overhead costs that a company has to cover on its way to profitability. Failing to identify and effectively address these shortcomings is like training for a race in the dark or solely in your mind. When nine out of ten companies don't make the journey from zero to twenty million in run rate, anyway that you can improve the odds of your company being the one out of ten has got to be taken seriously.

If you at all buy into the proposition that 'knowledge is power', it seems to me that you are forced to look at the question of 'what do I know and how am I sure that I actually know it'. (If you don't think that you are, then a career in the ministry might be more appropriate … where the proposition that 'believing is power' dominates). In business, knowledge always trumps belief.

When you use these assessment tools, unwarranted presumption gets caught in the headlights. You need to be ready to have your mistakes highlighted and your invincibility brought into open question. But you also have to be ready to find the 'golden ways' forward for your company … ways that you might never have thought of unassisted. The future of your company and its people has to trump all of those personal risks and more.

~~~~~~~~~~

Assessment Programs – High-Value Investments

With cutthroat competition in the global trade, businesses are working hard to break out of ruts. Many industries are popping up from nowhere to compete in the global market. Competition is getting tougher and companies are working smarter or falling behind.

Management assessment is a critical tool in this effort to stay ahead of the pack. Corporations that implement assessment programs are achieving tangible results and dominance in global trade. By a systematic use of questionnaires, exercises and interviews to assess and improve performance, companies are making better use of their key resources. In the better programs, questionnaires are interspersed with oral and written information from the interviewees.

The better the management assessment program works; the better will be the improvements in operating results. The assessment team carefully interprets and cross checks the data then recommends avenues for improvement. The value of the assessment depends on quality of the data collected. Once the data has been analyzed, the assessment team presents the report to CEO and Board of the company. In my experience, these assessment reports are one of the most valuable resources that management can have in its efforts to improve performance and outperform the competition.

Management assessment helps in locating the exact reasons for poor performance and support the development of an action plan for improvements. The management assessment provides a solid baseline for this action and subsequent assessments serve to monitor progress. Management assessments are useful for a range of other reasons:

- To prepare second line of defense i.e. selection or promotion of man power to critical roles: succession planning
- To identify developmental needs and direct the plan of action
- To provide space for plateau managers
- To identify and deal with reasons for performance problem
- To act as a guide to reorganize the present system
- To assess the adaptability to organizational changes
- To setup leadership mentoring sessions to improve performance

I have organized management assessments and assessment programs for a number of companies. The result is always the same – it is like turning the lights on in a darkened room. Assessment programs develop a very useful clarity and allow management to see clearly the challenges that it faces. One of my clients told me that the assessment program had saved her company untold hours of wasted time. "Before you set up our assessment program," she said "we used to waste hours debating what the problems were. We never had much time left over to work on the solutions. Your assessments lay the challenges out for us during the first hour of the session. We have nothing left to do but work on the solutions."

Assessment programs can literally make the difference between winning and losing in the race against your competition. Given their relatively modest cost and high value return, it makes good business sense have an assessment program running from the very beginning. To not do so is like running through a dark room filled with furniture – hard on the shins and not much else.

<u>Charting the Course – Crossing the Boundary</u>

A common weakness of almost all management theories is that they are an essentially static conception of a dynamic process. As such they cultivate ignorance rather than enlightenment and promote failure rather than success.

A couple of years ago I began a mentoring engagement with a CEO of an emerging company. As with all similar efforts it began with a search for one or two starting points – tactical issues – that we could initially focus on. But, it quickly became apparent that there was a large elephant in the room – one issue which seemed to overshadow all the others.

"I don't know what it takes to lead. And I don't know if I have the experience and wisdom to lead the team that we are forming. My company is growing faster than I am. I feel like

I'm being left behind – becoming less and less relevant."

This person had assembled a team and built a small but growing business. Their annual revenues had finally moved above a million dollars. That alone would seem an indication of the team's success and a validation of the company's value proposition. The business was moving out of the garage stage. Their client base was expanding. Things had finally started to look better after a long hard slog. But growing pains were emerging everywhere. And some of them were precursors of potentially very destructive problems.

The early stages of the company's growth were dominated by a group of people who were heavily involved in the technology that was at the root of the company's value proposition. But now the founders found themselves increasingly consumed by the problems of running and resourcing a business and out of touch with the latest technology developments. The expansion of the management team was producing cliques.

Original team members were increasingly coming up against problems that they lacked the skill set for and had no experience solving. New team members seemed to be expecting a more professional corporate culture than they found once on board and had little passion for the sense of family that had defined the earlier stages. The business development team looked more like an afterthought – an add-on – and seemed, in some ways, to be a whole other organization.

In the early days it was enough that the founder had a good idea and was passionate about the business, was a good salesman, great at making contacts and reliably getting business through the front door. It also helped that he could roll up his sleeves and deliver quality work to a satisfied client. But the first rush of growth was now in the past and things had started to deteriorate. The role the CEO had historically played left huge patches uncovered. Critical needs in the management area were taking time away from keeping current on the latest technology developments. The CEO was no longer the top technology ace in the stable.

There were challenges in these new areas that seemed intractable. Problems could no longer easily be diagnosed and solutions were much more difficult to devise and implement. Resourcing was a much more complicated matter and 'getting it wrong' was much more expensive. Simply said, there wasn't a process in place, any structure, any management, any data, and often insufficient records to allow him and his team to deal with them.

Taken together these growing pains and new challenges threatened to limit or block the company's growth. And the CEO, at first frustrated, was now becoming frightened that it was all going to fall apart despite his best efforts.

"I have assembled all these very talented people but I cannot seem to get them to work as a team and execute our corporate vision."

I had reservations about starting with such a complex set of issues. This is pretty heavy lifting for a first focus of a mentoring engagement. The CEO's apparently simple statement rested on top of a complex and interrelated set of problems. Here are just some of the issues that came to mind. The first was, of course, "What does it mean to lead?" The second was, "How does the process of evolving and promulgating a corporate vision have to change as a company grows?" The third focused on the question "How do you integrate increasingly diverse backgrounds and expectations into a rapidly growing team?" Another set of questions revolved around "What do I as a CEO have to become to effectively manage this new team?" And those were just some of the big issues! I suggested that we start with a more manageable focus. But the CEO was insistent that we start where his pain was the strongest. And so we headed for the mountain!

Over the following months I introduced a number of concepts that we eventually integrated into a holistic response to the core questions. The CEO undertook a heroic, and I say with some pride a successful, effort at changing his own behavior, ideas about leadership and understanding of how teams grow and work effectively. I am convinced that, without this work, the company would have languished and then declined – eventually going out of business. But the actual story is far brighter and the success far sweeter because of the concerted efforts that went into making the telling differences. The chronicles of our journey would fill a book. Here are just two examples of what we came up with:[1]

Re-envision yourself and your company: In some very important ways your company is like your child – and children grow up and, in the process, change. As much as you might, during nostalgic moments, like your teenager to have the needs and responses that they had when they were a five year old, treating them like a five year old is a sure recipe for disaster. At sixteen they need different things from you and, as a good parent; you need to make sure that they get them. It is much the same with your company.

In the early stages it needed you, as a founder, to be an invincible jack of all trades – a worker among a team of other workers who were laboring in support of its future – in many ways a leader among a group of relative contemporaries. Like the three year old it needed a god that is omnipotent – one that is always looking out for its interest and protecting it from the bad guys. As its father or mother you set the rules and made all the major (and sometimes minor) decisions. The company's needs were modest and you could provide them out of your own understanding, knowledge and emotional resources.

But as the company grew it needed you to become more

and more a manager who can bring in all sorts of talent and resources – and organize and manage them effectively. There is a reversal of the 'provider' roles. Your company is well on its way to becoming a better generator of economic benefits to a wider range of people than you could ever be. Much like a teenager develops their own taste in clothing and music, your company develops a culture that is different, and often radically different, than the one you tried to give it at birth.

Maybe another 'family' parable will help you see what I'm getting at. When you were single you got to determine pretty much everything about your life. Once you got married or into a 'significant other' relationship, things got a bit more complicated. Once you had two or three children and they started to grow into teenagers, things got completely out of hand. Your family took on a character that was neither you nor the sum of its members. It became a thing unto itself with its own characteristics, quirks and appetites.

So the challenge of growing a company into its teens is really a double one. Much like the parent relating to a child, you need to see to your own development while supporting the growth of your company. The two are connected in a vital way and, should they get out of phase, dysfunction is almost guaranteed.

Your first step is learning to be an effective parent of a teenager who is eager to become a young adult – then an adult in their own right. If you are going to be the person that facilitates this perilous journey, you must see to your own intellectual and emotional growth. Central to this process is developing a new understanding of what your company has become and is becoming. It is not the five year old that you had become comfortable with. There is rebelliousness about it and an urge for growth and exploration that was completely alien to the youngster. There is a drive for dominance and an aversion to being dominated. You must come to see it as it is – not as you wish it to be. You can no longer tell it was it is – you must let it tell you what it wants to become. You can no longer tell it what it needs – you must let it tell you what it needs.

Beyond that you must develop the skills and understandings necessary to play an increasingly supporting role effectively. Your role as 'god of the tribe' is coming to an end. You need to come to see your company, its value proposition and needs, in an entirely new way. You must pay attention to what your teenager is becoming on the way to adulthood. And if you don't give it what it needs … well ever had a frustrated teenager in the house?

Your company must traverse the storms and shoals of adolescence on the way to adulthood. As it does you will need to become less a father and more an advisor – you will have to become less a setter of the rules and more subject to them. There will be team members who know far better than you what is appropriate and effective in a particular situation. You need to give them the lead and follow that lead with the rest.

A company on a steep growth curve – like a teenager in the midst of full hormonal flush – needs parenting that has matured and adapted. As a CEO you cannot tolerate poor performance – either from yourself or from others. You need to raise your standards and expectations. You can no longer accept performance at prior levels.

The company is becoming potent in its own right and, as a result, can do more significant damage if it responds without discipline and careful training. Set the standards for performance and you will get what you accept. I saw a company die overnight because it lost its major source of business principally because the CEO could not bring herself to insist on a higher level of proposal development and review. The client, expecting a more professional proposal, was disappointed and went elsewhere. The company lost its base and reduced staff by 80% within the course of two months. It is no longer in business.

You must also redefine the corporate culture's standards for measuring success. As the old saw goes, 'amateurs practice until they get it right, professionals practice until they can't get it wrong.' You must professionalize your corporate culture and drive out the amateurish tendencies.

The good old days when good enough was acceptable are gone. You need to replace nostalgia for the good old days with professionalism and anticipation for the bright new future. In the past success may have meant winning a small purchase order – but now the chunks of business need to be larger and small purchase orders are a net loss for the company. Maybe in the past the Lone Ranger was the norm but now increasingly concerted and well-coordinated group action is required. The town now has a school, a couple of churches, two or three banks – and the whore houses have been driven beyond the city limits. The Lone Ranger has become a liability.

Your company must cultivate, and put a premium on, open communication and pluralism. More than one perspective will be involved in most major decisions. People have to know that they not only have the right but the responsibility to contribute to debates that effect the company's (and by derivation, theirs and your) future. I know of one company that rewards an employee for 'saving our butts on that one'. As you company grows more and more decisions will have the potential of causing greater and greater losses if made incorrectly. A critical part of your role is to set the conditions so that all relevant voices are heard and considered.

I often tell clients that, as their company grows, they have to avoid avoidance. Companies fail every year because the founders have an aversion to talking about, let alone resolving, a particular set of issues. One of the most common is a founder who continually talks about taking the company to a hundred million but is really very comfortable with a run rate in the high teens. I call these 'life style companies'. It is easy to recognize this person. They are usually high on one or another or the latest management theories, actively involved in one or another 'CEO groups' and busy moving the flatware around on the table. But over time you notice that nothing much is happening and the company seems to be languishing in a zone. So what are the names of the twin elephants in the room that the founder is so carefully avoiding? Most often they are 'can't delegate' and 'must control'. If you look carefully, the founder is acting as if the title CEO means chief of everything. The organization structure (no matter how hierarchical it looks on the org chart) is very flat. Look in the mirror. If this is you then you need to address rather than avoid.

But even if you evolve in the way your company needs you to, there are some things that you will never be able to give it.

Bring in Mentors: The great mythologist Joseph Campbell was fond of saying that "a father cannot be a mentor to his own son because they are both interested in the same woman." Of course, Sophocles had a bit of a jump on him and that Greek playwright gleaned that bit of human wisdom from myths that were centuries old when he wrote Oedipus, Rex.[2] But the lesson applies to your relationship to your company as well. There are some things that you can't do for your company and team. But those things need to be done – and you need to make sure that the right kinds of people are doing them.

Here, maybe a short story would help. Several years back I organized an annual all-hands retreat for a company. We took the entire crew on a three day Bahamas cruise.[3] We had over three hundred people in the group. Two of the days were at sea and the employees, management and board participated in a full schedule of meetings. The third day was on a private island. One of the organized events was a volleyball tournament. Teams were formed. I suggested to the CEO that he should not participate – let the rest of the group enjoy the event – but he couldn't. The result was predictable – his team won and the employees got an experience that was closer to the work environment than a fun day of casual competition. Sometimes you have to step out of the picture and let the cruise director organize things for the rest of the team!

One lesson here is that your senior team will benefit from chances to work together to meet your standards better if they don't have to beat you in the process. But a second, and far more important, lesson is that you can help your people succeed beyond their wildest dreams if you arrange for mentors – senior and very experienced resources – which they can connect with and learn from. This process begins with the very important realization that you are not the repository of all senior knowledge in the world and that others can mentor your people better. Once you are over that limiting delusion thinks can really begin to change for the better.

I build advisory boards as business development engines. Their principal purpose is to allow a company to access decision makers at a much higher level and to pursue and win lucrative business in much larger chunks. But, early on, I noticed a side benefit of the boards. They were made up of five to a dozen very experienced and well-connected individuals whose careers had spanned the entire range of challenges. During the early meetings of the board and as the members came into contact with the management team, mentoring relationships often began to develop almost at once. A CEO who was struggling with the problem of establishing a brand for his company was able to learn from an adviser who had built a very large and successful company from scratch. An SVP of business development learned about how his potential clients were really making their decisions from one who had been an insider for over a decade. A COO learned about best practices from someone who had spent decades perfecting them rather than a hired consultant who had a theory about how they should work. Over the years I have seen these kinds of things happen over and over again. Almost as if something that is lacking in our society at large is supplied by these mentors with astounding results. Here is the long and short of it: each of your senior people is going to benefit from a mentor in their field.

The experiences from this one mentoring engagement could fill a book. One day perhaps they will. Over the three years that it lasted, we were able to restructure the company twice, significantly professionalize its corporate culture and massively improve its resourcing. The lessons learned – such as the ones described above – have been used over and over in subsequent engagements. I hope that they will prove useful to you.

[1] This particular client was a strong family man. He and his wife had raised three kids who were in their mid-teens. Using his family experience helped him understand the complex challenges that his company was facing. Hence the heavy use of 'family metaphors' in what follows.
[2] By the way, before some of you get riled up about sexism, the same rule applies to the relationship between a daughter and her mother – only, in that case, they are interested in the same man!
[3] Now, don't knock it until you've tried it. I have been putting groups on cruise ships for over a decade – everything from board meetings, to strategic planning sessions and annual all-hands retreats. It is higher impact, much easier to organize, far less expensive and by far easily the best way to organize these events. If you don't believe me, send me an e-mail and I'll prove it to you.

~~~~~~~~~~

Crossing the Boundary – Surviving the Experience

It's seldom the dog that you love that bites you
It's almost always the one you can barely tolerate.

Many companies fail for reasons that have little to do with their core product or service. It is often the afterthoughts or 'under-thoughts' that cause failure when success has been looming on the horizon.

Companies with cutting-edge technologies are regularly beaten by those with more conventional ones – organizations with first rate value propositions find themselves losing to others which do not meet their high standards. The world can seem patently unfair – until you look at the competition – and the competition with the competition – differently.

Evolutionary Ideas

Early in my career as a recidivist entrepreneur I learned, sometimes by the hardest methods, that the business of business is different from the business of the business. You may want to go back and re-read that sentence a couple of times and sort it out before going any further but I will try, in what follows, to show you clearly what I mean.

When a company first comes into existence it is most likely that the entire senior team is composed of individuals who are minor variations on a common pattern. (Age, education, experience, ethnicity, interests, etc.) They are comfortable with each other and that goes a long way towards developing the spirit of intense camaraderie that is necessary for any initial success. Each team member may assume (or be assigned) a unique role within the team and company but it is their underlying common characteristics that dominate and define the initial corporate culture.

In the early years a company grows by turning the connections of senior team members, often most notably the CEO's, into an initial client base. Sometimes this may be possible because some of the senior team have recently left a company which subsequently becomes a client. At other times potential clients may have been supportive of the team's intentions to launch the company. But, however it occurs, companies which survive the initial stages of growth do so because they have generated, and then cultivated, an initial client base which helps them turn a burn rate into a run rate.

During this stage, corporate functions are serviced either by founders (making it up as they go along) or by narrowly experienced personnel in the business disciplines. So the HR function is managed by a good recruiter and the financial system is handled by a controller. Some of these functions may be outsourced either partially or completely during the early years. The business of business takes a back seat to the business of the business.

The Dogs You Don't Like

As a company grows in size and complexity the requirements in these 'business of business' areas become more critical to its success. Mistakes or errors have more serious implications. The journey from burn rate to run rate – from draining away financial resources to significant levels of net income – is a difficult one for most companies but, once achieved, many companies find themselves in completely uncharted territory and suffering from extreme vertigo.

However this transition is managed, a company enters into uncharted waters when it moves into the black.

Companies that manage this transition effectively enter a new evolutionary phase. The transition is non-linear – change is quantum. Some of the characteristics of a start-up are left behind. For instance, they cease being 'science projects' and begin the serious journey towards becoming a fully functioning company. They enter onto a path that, with skill, dedication, persistence, wisdom and more than a fair share of luck, may lead their 'science projects' towards corporate maturity.

In these early months and years management can mostly provide for the needs of the growing company by sticking close to the 'dog they love'. By this I mean that, if the company is involved in a particular technology or service, close connection with that technology or service permeates the corporate culture and defines the experience of team members – a gathering of similars. But success and growth brings its own set of issues.

At some point the company's needs for further growth exceeds the senior management team's ability to generate new clients and expand the business base. Around this time other – management – issues such as an increasing need for appropriately qualified people to service client's needs and a rising appetite for financial resources begins to push the management team's attention towards those 'dogs that they can barely tolerate'.

Evolutionary Pressures

It is at this critical juncture that two fundamental rules of evolution come into play. The first is 'evolution or extinction'. Organisms – including companies and CEOs – have to continue evolving as the requirements of the environment they find themselves in change. Without appropriate evolutionary responses to these changes, increasing irrelevance then disappearance defines the future. The second rule is 'your excess will limit the impact of your excellences'. Aversions have a tendency to produce such excesses. Ignoring a need assiduously, for instance, is such an excess. Aversions lead to conflicts – among the senior team and between the team and the evolving needs of the company. It is these conflicts – completely tangential to either the growth of the company or its evolving needs – more often than inadequacies in the value proposition – that bring down companies.

During this time of transition the culture of the company, along with the core skill sets that have made up the senior management team, begins to undergo a substantial distortion – as an attempt to meet the new needs comes into conflict with the limitations imposed by the 'old order'. Seen one way, this distortion is actually a movement towards generally accepted business practices and requires recognition that the business of business is becoming more nearly as important as the business of the business. Seen another way it is a threat to 'traditions' within the emerging company. CEOs and the senior team will either participate in or oppose these pressures. Their decisions, as much as the competition, will determine the company's future.

Natural Selection – Surviving the Barrier

Evolutionary pressures tend to, over time, weed out weak and inappropriate behaviors in favor of the strong and relevant. The awful physics of the process can often seem inhuman and arbitrary. But arguments over its humanity or arbitrary nature are red-herrings. Where survival is the imperative, evolutionary accommodation is the only effective response.

So, what does survival mean in this situation? It means appropriate responses to the pressures for growth. It also means that there are real penalties incurred for inappropriate responses to those pressures. Let me provide an example of the later in order to bracket the term 'appropriate'. Faced with this challenge, many CEOs embark on an 'educational journey' to become more sophisticated in one or more functional business areas. Two of the most common are finance and marketing. They seek to become better at these disciplines than the people they have hired. While laudable, this is essentially a reaction to an aversion – a distancing from the 'dogs they can barely tolerate' – a distraction from the fundamental challenge that they, as CEOs, face. The company's needs are changing as it grows. The CEO and senior team need to evolve in order to meet those changing needs – and change can be a difficult proposition even without the pressures of building a company.

Surviving the journey through the barrier has more to do with the maturing of individual senior team members than with the accumulation of additional specific skills sets. Becoming 'appropriate' as a leader of a growing company begins with matching that maturation process with that of the company. As adolescents do not tend to do well in adult environments, immaturity in a CEO will, more effectively than almost any other trait, limit the future of the company.

For a CEO, the challenge of evolving along with a growing company can be a daunting one. But, as uncomfortable as that journey might be, the alternative – holding back the company until it finally expires from exhaustion and frustrated aspirations – should motivate any CEO to 'take the bull by the horns' and prevail over their own limitations.

~~~~~~~~~~

The Propose of a Compass

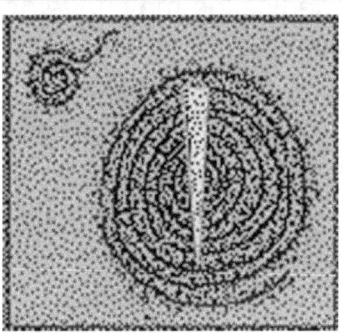

~~~~~~

It's not the compass that finds your true north – you need to find <u>the compass</u> that points to your true north. Short of that, every other compass will send you in the wrong direction.

~~~~~~~~~~~~~~~~~~~~~~

Life mentoring can bring some of life's grandest adventures. The issues at stake are often monumental and, not infrequently, the results can be life changing. In current times such mentoring is frequently requested by individuals at the very crossroads of their careers. One such engagement began not long ago.

I often receive requests for initial consultations from people who have recently found their current employment untenable. Sometimes they simply have decided that a change is required. Perhaps a yearning for greener pastures or a feeling that there has to be something more to life drives them to seek me out. Maybe they have followed a path to its end – or, at least, a plateau – and find that there is less to be enthusiastic about. Life has a way of bringing us all to those times and places. Others have had their place disturbed by economic developments or decisions by their superiors. Years of work and dedication may have gone into a position that was abruptly terminated.

Initial consultations tend to run according to a pattern – and, if I am able, the person leaves with significantly more than anticipated. Let me tell you a story.

I was recently approached by an executive who had spent a great deal of time, energy and personal resources working with a company that was, by all appearances, very poorly served by its founder. There is a lot of the going around – as there ever is. As a result, he had found his way to an ending that put financial pressure on him and his family. But the biggest blow was to his sense of self-esteem and confidence. He could not believe that he had allowed himself to be put in such a position.

Prior to our session, he had sought out friends and asked their assistance in re-launching his career. The advice he received was predictable. "Pull together a resume. Highlight your accomplishments. Focus on the impacts that you were able to contribute." He had even gone so far as to draft a new resume plus a number of collateral documents. As our meeting began, he laid out his strengths and began to describe the kind of position he was seeking – his description went into great detail. I brought his 'elevator speech' to an abrupt halt with a simple question.

"If you could do anything that you wished, what would give you the greatest satisfaction?"

You see, he was falling into the classical trap of seeing his next step along life's journey as a minor variation on the ones that went before. More to the point, he was focusing on the skills that he had developed and was looking for a way to put them to work. In the past he had been an architect of sorts – designing and building solutions to hard problems. But here he was extolling his skill with a hammer.

What was missing – what made his presentation almost soulless – was a sense of joyous anticipation that would be a sign of pursuing something larger than himself. He had a compass but not a north star – not a sense of his own 'true north'.

You see, a compass is worthless without such a thing. It is not that a compass has a purpose – it is what it proposes that is important. To quote Yogi Berra, "if you don't know where you are going, how will you know when you get there?" the very meaning of a compass requires such a thing as true north.

Finding True North

As we talked, I kept leading the conversation back to those times he felt he had found his true north. Soon he was describing two times in his life that he had made important contributions through his understanding, insight, persistence and dedication. Neither of these was insignificant. As he talked, he began to get more and more enthusiastic – more and more excited as he described the work and the feelings that came with solving problems – meeting challenges – that others found too daunting.

As we circled back to his current situation and mindset, several things began to come clear. The first was that he was too involved in the details of getting his next job to take the time to think about my question. To say it another way, he was too busy driving to have any time to stop for gas! As a result, he was thinking tactically about a strategic decision. The second was that he had allowed the pressure he was feeling to keep him from thinking about the alternatives which he clearly had. In fact, it is fair to say that he was too much about thinking and not enough about dreaming. The third was that his recent experience had tested his self-confidence to the point that he had forgotten those past successes. Finally, he had been seeking direction from his friends and business network when the real answer to my question was within himself.

The last half of our session was very different from the first. We talked about how he might free his mind from the tensions that were clouding his vision – small things that he could do for himself that would free up the dreaming and allow it to flower. It seemed to me that there was more opportunity before him than he was seeing – and, as we talked, he came to see that as true.

A Most Daunting Question

On the face of it, the core question seems relatively harmless. But most people spend a lot of time and energy avoiding it. "What is it that makes you happiest to do?" Early on, a friend told me, "find out what you really enjoy doing and do it as much as possible. It is the only thing that you have any chance of being really good at." But the first attempts at answering such a question were very tentative – almost as if I was afraid of finding the answer. It seems silly that such a simple but important piece of self-knowledge should be so off-putting. I suppose philosophers and psychiatrists would chalk it up to a feeling of inadequacy. But the journey towards its answer is one of the most important ones that any human being makes – and it is a terrible shame to die before the answer is in hand.

The truly devilish part of all of this is that the answer – the definition of you own 'true north' – is within you right now. It is calloused over by all those things your parents, friends and teachers told you should be important – should be central to what you are and will become. It is not a matter of asking others – it is a matter of asking yourself. Maybe this will help:

Advice by Bill Holm

Someone dancing inside us

learned only a few steps:

the 'Do your work' in 4/4 time

the 'What do you expect' waltz

He hasn't noticed yet the woman

standing away from the lamp,

the one with black eyes

who knows the rumba,

and strange steps in jumpy rhythms

from the mountains of Bulgaria.

If they dance together,

something unexpected will happen.

If they don't, the next world

will be a lot like this one.

Find the Answer – Your Life Hangs in the Balance

It is so incredibly easy to let life flow away – not to wring the sweet marrow out of it – to find the true gift that it brings. Life can become that of an oxen – a domesticated animal condemned to pulling someone else's wagon along a path that they have chosen. But that is not life – that is existence. It is surely a path from cradle to grave. But what a wasteful path it is.

Each of us has been granted a span of years. Each has a new chance every day we are alive to find our own personal true north. None of us is born with a map that shows us the way to those paths of fulfillment and joyous celebration of life. Without our own deliberate effort, it is much more likely that we will take the oxen's path. The time for that effort is ever now – in the moment before you – not in the moment to come. You become because of what you decide – the moment to come is too late.

There is great joy in finding those paths – and in helping others find theirs. Nothing else that a human can accomplish comes close to that value – not wealth, health or salvation. Finding and following our paths that lead to our own 'true north' is what humans are made for – it is close to the very meaning of life.

~~~~~~~~~~~

When Opposites Detract

There are lessons to learn from listening to what people say – and sometimes those lessons go well beyond what has been said.

~~~~~~~~~~~~~~~~~~~~~

Some 90% plus Americans say they believe in heaven and hell. That corrosive Zoroastrian legacy leaches into their civil society and world view. I suspect that the French have a better handle on this – less than half say they believe in heaven but more than two-thirds believe in hell!

Americans generally are addicted to an adolescent bilateral-symmetry. This simple-minded tendency leads them to see most things in black and white. Under its oppressive ideology, the opposite of anything is named by simply attaching an 'un' to it. The opposite of 'clear' becomes 'unclear'. The opposite of 'ambiguous' becomes 'unambiguous'. But what suffices for adolescents is often insufficient for adults. While the opposite of clear may occasionally be unclear, the opposite of ambiguous is rarely unambiguous.

Intentionality

The idea that words have denotative meanings becomes a somewhat unwieldy concept as a 'silly-putty' language like American leads many to the presumption that intention need only emerge proximately. This tendency is often over-glossed by the constant 'guilty but with an explanation' plea that characterizes most American writers.

These are authors who constantly have to explain what they meant to people they assume 'just didn't get it'. Their writings seem to require a compensating companion – a continuing further explanation and clarification. But this, of course, does not ever suffice. Language should stand on its own and not require more than it is. Language should be intentionally clear. Less than that is a lack of clarity and that is worse than unclear – it is insulting.

A writer should accept that at least a portion of readers should be capable of understanding complex ideas couched in subtle uses of language. Otherwise, why bother – go read Shakespeare to a cockroach! Adolescences all around provides a delightful opportunity for the uninformed to lecture the unwilling on how to do the unnecessary. And, although some authors seem to prefer such a thing, is truth is it simply a kamikaze raid on a vacant lot – a waste of the possibility of actually awakening alive.

Clarity begins with intentionality. Intentionality is grounded in carefully crafted purposefulness. Writing without intentionality and purposefulness is much more like a finger painting by a three year old than a van Gogh or Picasso – more like Mozart than Beethoven – more akin to scrapple than pâté de foie gras.

The opposite of intentionality is indolence and indolence produces faux ambiguity. Extended adolescence produces an aversion to ambiguity. As the temporally-challenged encounter adult conceptions, they insist that there always has to be beginnings and middles and endings. Adults, of course, accept that it is all 'middles'. You are born into an ongoing conversation and are obliged to leave before it is ended.

But these Three-Card-Monte types are insistent and, even with an occasional shuffling of this limited deck; there is always a bright colored tag on each. They don't want to slip up and lose track, you know.

Ambiguity is most certainly an adult predilection and, like a taste for well-aged whiskey, steak tartar, caviar or a fine cigar, it is a maturing prerogative that requires an acquiring mind.

The opposite of ambiguity may sometimes be aversion. Faux clarity often signals an aversion to ambiguity and a tendency towards faux ambiguity. Clarity – which reduces reality to binary options – characters are good or bad – situations dire or idyllic – endings are happy or sad – and the reader is either Mutt or Jeff – is, first and foremost, a comment on the maturity of the author. Whatever ends up on the page speaks first about the author – their wisdom, courage, determination, purposefulness and intentionality – or lack thereof – and only belatedly to the subject being addressed.

For children ambiguity is always an irritation. To speak to a child in a way that holds their attention, ambiguity needs to be scrubbed out of the text. But for adults, ambiguity is delicious – scintillating – seductive. The warm rush of the intentionally imprecise has set many a heart racing.

~~~~~~~~~~~~~~~~~~~~

She dressed as if there was something delicious to hide – never exposing much – or encasing herself in a dump of denim, burlap and bulk – but as if there was something strongly feminine – mysterious and sensual –that might be exposed if the right rhythms kidnapped her heart's beating. And that made her incredibly dangerous.

~~~~~~~~~~~~~~~~~~~~

A man pays no compliment to a woman when he tells her she's beautiful. Either she is, and knows it – in which case he has stated the obvious and is boring – or she is not and knows it – in which case he is deluded and inconvenient. What she really wants is to hear is that she makes him nervous – better yet, that he's afraid of her. As well he should be. Perhaps he is a man to her woman. At least then something would be possible.

~~~~~~~~~~~~~~~~~~~~~~

Ambiguity is not the lack of intentionality – it is far more intentional that the unambiguous. The opposite of ambiguity is not clarity it is adolescence – faux clarity. The antidote for faux clarity is maturity – a richer and cumulative life experience and a more subtle understanding of life and the other.

Multiplication

As life's experience advances, what was binary becomes increasingly complex. The two (clarity and ambiguity) become four (clarity, non-clarity, ambiguity, non-ambiguity) in an attempt to maintain the model. Then the four become eight (clarity, non-clarity, precision, indolence, ambiguity, non-ambiguity, adolescence, maturity) plus one (bilateral symmetry) which makes nine. The sensibility of it all becomes strained and the interloper looks increasingly dog-eared.

In a moment that is often forever life changing, the linear becomes something else altogether. The strip of paper is twisted half a turn and attached back to itself. A Möbius strip is formed dissolving the once over-arching principal of bilateral-symmetry into meaninglessness.[1] Once freed from this straightjacket, the eight dissolve into fluidity – unpaired and with two new organizing principles (asymmetric relationalism and multi-dimensional intentionality) washing over them.

Opposites Detract

The world of human experience is neither bilateral nor symmetrical. To insist that it is indicates a preference for faux experience – that the world wears a mask and hides its true face. But, more insidiously, it constitutes a determined preference for the artificial over authentic experience. Synthetic judgments a priori that are useful within most professional disciplines are corrosive of the living human experience. They may make a better chemist or mechanic but they will proscribe experiencing the richness and diversity that life has to offer.

---

[1] A model of a Möbius strip can be constructed by joining the ends of a strip of paper with a single half-twist. A line drawn starting from the seam down the middle will meet back at the seam but at the "other side". If continued the line will meet the starting point and will be double the length of the original strip of paper. This single contiguous curve demonstrates that the Möbius strip has only one boundary.

If the strip is cut along the above line, instead of getting two separate strips, it becomes one long strip with two full twists in it, which is not a Möbius strip. This happens because the original strip only has one edge which is twice as long as the original strip of paper. Cutting creates a second independent edge, half of which was on each side of the knife or scissors. Cutting this new, longer, strip down the middle creates two strips wound around each other.

~~~~~~~~~~

Eleven Habits of Self-Sabotaging People

If you are depressed,
you are living in the past.
If you are anxious,
you are living in the future.
If you are at peace,
you are living in the present.

- Lao Tzu

This chapter has its roots in a chance conversation with an old friend. He shook his head and wondered why one of his employees kept acting in ways that sabotaged his own interests. It got me to wondering – then asking – then asking some more. This is a journey inward as much as outward. After all, none of us are exempt from being human.

~~~~~~~~~~~~~~~~~~~~

I've been a student of human behavior for at least four decades. During that time I've become fascinated by behaviors which people adopt and which are self-sabotaging. Over the years I have developed a list of these behaviors which I used to keep track of the tendencies of people that I met. [Have you noticed that there seem to be a lot more self-sabotaging in the world? I have.] I recently began to suspect that the percentage in American society was shifting even more towards the negative tendencies. My natural curiosity – as well as my damaged sense of national pride – led me to do a bit of research.

In my advisory work I teach clients to open files on each person they meet and keep a record of their experiences with them. This keeps them from wasting time with non-productive relationships. Recently I have received a number of requests for some sort of organized presentation of the system. [There were it seems other people who were having the same experiences] I set about to formalize the list and provide a guide for using it. I even developed a 'point system' that seems to work remarkably well. [Everybody starts out with a hundred points. Points are deducted for each transgression.] I came up with eleven habits of self-sabotaging people. Here is the list:

1. They Are Late: I consider this unthinking treatment of others (and me in particular) to be one of the seminal indicators of a lack of respect. Being on time is one of the easiest ways to indicate to a person that their time and the potential relationship are important to you. It is also one of the easiest compliments to pay. You simply arrive on schedule.

Self-sabotaging people are almost always late for meetings. Somehow they don't seem to recognize the incredibly insulting nature of this behavior. *"Your time is so unimportant that I do not need to conserve it. You will see me when I get there. Until then, you wait!"* seems to be the prevailing attitude. This, of course, quickly translates into *"You are barely worth my time and should be happy that I showed up at all."*

When confronted with the insulting nature of this behavior these people usually come up with something like *"I am sorry. My schedule always seems to get out of control. I am a victim of my own celebrity."* This replaces one insult with another – *"You are not worth it"* becomes *"You are the true victim of my incompetency. It is your burden to bear."* Of course you are then asked to believe that they are going to prove completely competent in other, more demanding areas. [Give me a break - minus ten points]

2. They Are Unprepared: I am constantly amazed at how little time self-sabotaging people spend preparing for meetings. As a matter of course, I prepare as if the individual that I am meeting is important and the matters we are going to discuss have substance.

My company's website provides a lot of information about my interests, core competencies and projects. We do that for a reason – so that people can go there and find out about us. I also publish a lot of articles on various subjects – again to help people know what my interests are and identify possible common interest. We go to a lot of effort to make that information available. So what does it say about a person when they come to an initial meeting without spending any significant time on the website? In other words, they are winging it!

Most often I have spent a fair amount of time on their site (including printing out selected portions to use at the meeting). Pages will have highlighted areas where I want clarification or additional information. I spend time going over things that either interested or confused me. Self-sabotaging people are generally not even conscious of the difference in our preparation levels. [Minus ten points]

3. They Are Unfocused: I get to a meeting and quickly discover that the other person has not thought through why he was interested in meeting with me. I remember meeting with a guy who had asked me to advise him on a new career direction. We set up a session to which he arrived late. [Minus ten points – I was doing him a favor and he returned it by insulting me] When we finally settled down and my temper came back under control, I asked him what he wanted to do – what direction he was considering. *"I really don't know,"* was the reply *"I've just started thinking about it."* I paid the check and left Bo Peep to find his sheep. [Minus twenty points – a double!]

4. They Are Superficial: *"I just wanted to meet with you to see if you could help me get business."* Wow, I love this one. When the hell did I become your business development department – and, if I understand you correctly, an unpaid one at that? Give me a break. And if you really want to bring the conversation to a complete halt, ask *"what's the quid pro quo".* Usually the response is something like *"Well, I'd be happy to pay you a finder's fee if I do get business from one of your introductions."* Sure, I'm likely to risk the time and reputation of one of my valued contact by introducing them to someone who is intent on wasting my time! [Minus ten points]

One more out of this particular barrel – I get a call from a person who has linked up with me through Linked In. She is traveling to the DC area and would like to explore a 'possible common interest'. She is very expansive in her vision of a possible common project. Some of what she says makes some sense. So we schedule a dinner. As the dinner starts it quickly becomes clear that she has read some crap by some networking guru that told her 'never to eat alone'. So she cooked up a shallow-water rationale. The meeting was totally unproductive – a complete waste of my time – but she did get to fulfill the author's proscription. Another friend of mine was subjected to exactly the same treatment by this person during the same visit to the area. [Minus twenty points – another double!]

5. They Are Uninformed: I work in a number of fairly focused spaces. I have accumulated quite a bit of knowledge, experience and some wisdom in those areas. So I am always a bit shocked when I am subjected to a monologue by somebody who clearly does not know what they are talking about. The oldest wisdom is that 'knowing what you don't know is far more important than knowing what you do.' But these people don't seem to have a clue. They prattle on and I glaze over. Maybe the time will go faster if I can fall asleep! Private ignorance is your own business but public ignorance is offensive to the people who are forced to sit through its display. [Minus ten points]

There is one variation of this tendency which I find particularly offensive. I have had people brazenly disrespect people that I know well – and that they know I know well. When I ask about their relationship it becomes clear that they don't know the person they are disparaging. What's the point? Does this self-sabotaging person really believe that I will cast aside a deeper relationship and disown a friend because of their uninformed and self-destructive behavior? What to they think I am going to think of them because of this? People who are convinced that ignorance is their best side are such a pain. [Minus ten points]

6. They Are Unaware: I call these people the situationally challenged. They don't seem to have any understanding of what a particular venue or occasion calls for. They plow on with their droning pitch oblivious of what is going on around them or the reactions of the people who are being forced to listen. The rest of the world seems to disappear for these people and, if I am not the focus of their monologue, that includes me. I am nobody's nobody! [Minus ten points]

There is one particular variation of this behavior which really boils my oil. I call it the one-lane highway syndrome. I maintain a very extensive mailing list and sometimes I get asked to send out notices of events. I will admit that I used to do so routinely as a friendly accommodation. But a number of experiences have caused me to rethink that response. Here is an example of what I mean:

A person who runs events was in the habit of asking me to inform my contacts about them. At first I complied but then something happened that changed my mind. I asked for support for an event that I had organized. The individual responded that, since a competing organization was part of the event, he couldn't support it. I realized that, should I have applied the same conditions, I would have not mailed out my notices. So I guess he saw me as a greater fool. Subsequently I requested another favor only to receive a variation of the same response. The message was clear – this is a one-lane highway and that lane runs from you to me! I owe you nothing in return for your consideration and support! [Minus twenty points]

7. They Are Inconsiderate: I have watched people cut out a third member in a group in order to drill down to what they obviously see as the 'golden fleece' – maybe the senior member of the group. Occasionally it has gotten so bad that I had to ask them to leave. I have seen people invade a private house and hijack a social occasion with an ideological tirade. I have seen guests disrespect their host and wonder why people find them repugnant. After all, aren't they just telling everybody the truth?

When something like this happens, I am reminded of A Light Woman – a poem by Robert Browning which observes:

> *'Tis an awkward thing to play with souls,*
> *And matter enough to save one's own*

These idiot-logues – these 'players-with-souls' – are to be avoided at all costs. Civility is a compliment easily given and almost always graciously received. Boorishness is just that – boorish. What an individual will do socially is a pale reflection of what they will do in business relationships. [Minus twenty points]

8. They are Ungrateful: I always keep a plus and minus account for each person that I have helped. This lets me identify, and then avoid, people who seem to think I am a vendor of goodies and that they have no responsibility to return the favor. You should begin to keep the same records. The first thing that you will discover is that with certain people your tendency to help is often responded to with a complete lack of gratitude and no interest at all in evening up accounts.

In his marvelous book *Rising Sun*, Michael Crichton has Captain John Connor talking with his junior partner Lt. Webster Smith. Connor mentions that another character once saved his life. Smith responds that Connor was being reminded of that. No, Connor replies, he would never do that. It is my obligation to remember.

People who need to be reminded to remember that you took the time and made the effort to help them should not be reminded they should be avoided. [Minus thirty points!]

One of the tendencies that I have is to put together people who I think might have common interests. Over the years I have made numerous introductions – some of which have lead to substantial amounts of business and significant relationships. For the most part these individuals repay my kindness by offering their support or introductions in areas that are important to me. But there is a small percentage that sees the contributions I make as a net benefit. I have even had a couple of these invite me to drinks and then ask "who else do you know that I should meet?" I always reply "Given my last experience with introducing somebody to you, why should I want to go through that completely unsatisfying process again?" The conversation tends toward a proclamation of exceptionalism – but it is over for me from the very beginning. At least I will get a drink out of it! [Minus twenty points]

9. They Are High Maintenance: We've all met this kind – or, shall I say, been subjected to them? Recently I had a meeting scheduled with a person who had contacted me suggesting collaboration on a rather major project. An hour before the meeting I received an e-mail asking if we could start half an hour later. I agreed – after all these things happen. I arrived at the restaurant on time only to wait for a further half an hour while this person navigated the four blocks from their hotel. Additionally she introduced a third individual into the meeting – contending that she had previously mentioned this person. She had, of course, not done so and the person was an irrelevant participant. It never seemed to occur to this person that she had just branded herself as an unreliable and disrespectful partner in any collaboration. First, the restaurant was an accommodation – chosen because it was close to her hotel. The delay in the start time was also an accommodation. And now my consideration was returned by subjecting me to this insulting behavior. And in the end this person was so socially unaware the she suggested that, after all her disrespectful behavior, that we split the check. [Minus thirty points]

Another of this type seems to think that a discussion of the challenges they face in delivering on their commitments is necessarily of interest to me. They go on and on about how difficult their life is and how much effort will be required to live up to their obligations under any agreement. When this starts happening, I generally close the book and move on. I will deliver on my obligations and deal with my challenges. I expect the other person to do the same. Instead they seem to want to make their problems, as well as mine, my burden. [Minus ten points]

Finally there are the types who seem to need a den mother to remind them of deadlines and obligations. You have to constantly be after them to deliver on their commitments. They see it as part of your obligation to do so. Thanks, but my life is complicated enough and you had a mother – I'm not yours now. [Minus ten points]

10. They Are Opportunistic: This behavior is decidedly predatory and easy to spot. Go to any 'networking' event and you will see them prowling around. They go from person to person with basically the same proposition. *"Hi, I'm so-and-so and I need this. Can you provide it?"* Nothing about who you are or even who they are – they apparently are only a need that you either can satisfy or become nothing to them.

I am a big believer in the proposition that whenever opportunity knocks it is best to open the door. My experience is also that opportunity will flee when confronted with an assault rifle or a lunge for the jugular. Most people, when approached by someone who is clearly not interested who they are – only in how they can be used to satisfy a need, are offended. Productive relationships are not built on predatory tendencies. [Minus ten points]

11. They Are Full of Hubris: I have saved this one for last because it is by far the most egregious behavior of self-sabotaging people. Hubris arises out of the cult of self-anointed-celebrity – individuals who have lost contact with the fact that they, like all of the rest of us, are human – that they are just as fallible as the rest of us – that they are going to die like the rest of us – and that they should respect others as they wish to be respected.

This type of person is an expert at the one-lane-highway proposition. It is, of course, their right to expect that things only move in one direction – from you to them. You are after all, their lesser! What could be more reasonable? So here is my question, why would you have anything to do with such a person? Because of what they could do for you! Grow up and smell the night-soil. They will never do anything for you – you will only do for them.

I organized a program that involved a panel. It was one of my 'cruise ship' programs – we ran it during a Caribbean cruise. I had scheduled a meeting with a person who had expressed an interest in the program and the panel. Prior to our meeting, I had supplied the brochure, URL address for the event website and a fairly detailed description of the mutually beneficial arrangements that we should focus on. So we met at this office. It quickly became clear that the only question on his mind was *"Am I on the panel?" "Well how about the quid pro quo suggestions,"* I replied? *"You should be happy that I have agreed to be on your panel. My name alone is enough contribution,"* was effectively the response. And this from a minor player from a mid-range firm. Such self-aggrandizement is butt ugly. [Minus fifty points]

Here is another one. I build advisory boards as business development engines. They are the most productive way I have ever found to turbo-charge the process. The boards are made up of four to seven highly experienced and connected individuals. Their job is to identify major chunks of new business and to assist the company to capture that business through a strong and persistent advocacy. Occasionally an individual is interviewed for board membership who is convinced that their presence on the board will be enough to draw new business in. They think that making introductions is enough. What is fascinating about these individuals is that they have combined a radical overestimation of their important with a massively delusional vision of the way business is actually done. [Minus fifty points]

Using the System My files get updated after each meeting, phone call or other experience. When a person's score drops below 80, I put them on the 'provisional' list. These are people I will do business with only if there is no other option with a higher score. When a person's score drops below 60, I let them know that I am not interested in dealing with them unless they can improve my experience with them. When the score drops below 50, I don't return calls.

Well, there it is. Give it a test drive and let me know what you think. Send me your stories – enter them in the comment box below. I would like to hear from you.

~~~~~~~~~~

Making the Possible Probable

When you awake each morning, the day presents you with literally thousands of possibilities. Human existence is chocked full of possibilities. But the important question is what is probable? And the more important question is, how can you make the right possible things probable – how can you select the right probabilities from all those possibilities? This is one of those areas when more education can be a real liability.

~~~~~~~~~~~~~~~~~~~~

Executive mentoring my way leads me to work with highly educated and literate people. Most of my clients have a Master's degree. In some ways, working with these people is a joy. For example, they have been trained to understand and work with complex ideas. Their grasp of the language is such that conversations about complex ideas are possible.

However, every coin has a reverse side. Facility with language and subtleties brings an increased skill in self-deception and denial of the obvious. Some things are better said – and understood – in plain language. An example might help you understand what I am getting at.

I was asked by the Chairman of a Board of Directors to work with the CEO. The company was a start-up that had made it through the initial stages and was pushing towards twenty million in annual revenue. The CEO had lead his team through several growth-generated reorganizations similar to the ones I described in <u>Battle at the Cottage Gate</u>. In the process, he had to reinvent himself a couple of times – as his role in the company changed in response to the new dynamics.

Recently the Chairman had become concerned. The company had reached a plateau of sorts and growth had started to level off. It wasn't so much the leveling off that bothered him – he had seen too much of business to expect that growth would continue without interruption – but the reaction of the CEO to the development.

The CEO had begun to withdraw into himself. He had become less communicative. When he did brief the board, his presentations were halting and poorly focused – quite out of character and not at all what the board had come to expect. The situation had caused some board members to begin to talk about succession. An informal succession committee had been formed and was talking about a search for a new CEO. Perhaps, the reasoning went, our present CEO had risen to the limit of his capabilities.

I took the engagement on the condition that nothing would be done by the board – either overtly or covertly – on the issue of succession for at least ninety days. The Chairman readily agreed but I pushed for a unanimous undertaking by all members of the board. Once that was in place, I was introduced to the CEO – let's call him John.

My first meeting with John lasted almost three hours. He was clearly frustrated by the resistance he was encountering. As he saw it, the resistance was coming from the team. John had laid down the challenge – break the twenty million dollar barrier – and the team, although they appeared to be trying, were not making real progress.

One problem became clear during this initial session. John was a very literate person who could weave plausible descriptions and explanations around even the most obtuse issues. He was mentally agile enough to quickly respond to any topic I would bring up and managed to talk with an authoritative air. Language was getting in the way of communication.

I noticed a tendency in John's behavior. He quickly occupied the intellectual 'high ground' as a strategy for controlling and dominating – channeling – the discussion. Talking to him about this tendency created a very interesting situation. His occupation of the high ground occurred more quickly and his defense of his position was more strident. Those of you with an interest in logical argument will probably see the problem – self-referencing discussions tend to be circular.

The difference in his reaction to this topic gave me a clue to the best way to advance the engagement. I focused the discussion on the question of the necessary evolution of a leadership style as a company grows. At first, John took the initiative and began to pontificate on leadership theory. But I doggedly turned the conversations back to the question of the evolution of John as a leader. It wasn't an easy maneuver but my persistence eventually overcame John's tendency to intellectualize the discussion.

Actually there were three entities in the room during our discussions – John, me and the company. My approach was that the company was growing up and its needs were changing as that occurred. John was clearly not fulfilling the needs of this new phase.

At first, John tried to turn the discussion to focus on the team and its inadequacies. But I would have none of it. The question on the table was leadership and the need for leadership to evolve to meet the evolving needs of the company. Things got a bit heated a couple of times but eventually we settled down to the discussion of John's leadership.

I was then that the core of the problem first raised its head. "I used to understand the challenges that came my way – I was always able to come up with solutions that I could pass along to the team – but now these new challenges are beyond me." Those of you who have lived through the growth of a child from toddler through adolescence then on to adulthood – particularly in the current environment of rapidly advancing technologies – will probably find more meaning in John's statement. He was feeling inadequate.

In ancient, traditional societies there was a rule about the integration of a young man or woman into the broader society – 'the rite of passage required a guide and neither the mother or father could serve that role". The great mythologist Joseph Campbell put it this way, "a boy's father cannot be his initiator because they are both interested in the same woman". The point here is that a 'responsible and experienced stranger' is required to lead the youth to adulthood.

Did that mean that the members of the board who had begun to talk of succession were right? This possibility clearly occurred to John. But that would be like suggesting that, once a youth was initiated into the adult part of a society, his father would have no relationship with him at all. The father's responsibility is to begin to see his son in a different light – as an adult – and to treat him that way. If John could make that journey, there would be no need for him to leave the tribe.

I'll tell the rest of the story – of the 'leap' the company took into an entirely new paradigm – in a later article but, for now, I want to finish the story of John's journey. Our sessions got tenser as the discussion turned from the intellectualized vision of leadership to John's. Overcoming the tendency to keep the conversation 'out there' – at arm's length – was very difficult for John. But, to his credit, John kept on even when things were very uncomfortable for him.

By the end of our sixth of seventh session, John began to realize that his vision of leadership was not evolving. His idea of what a leader had to be was adequate to the early-stage challenges. But these new ones were far more complex. The tool was not up to the task. Central to this realization was the idea that complex tasks required coordinated efforts if solutions were going to be found. His tendency to quickly occupy the intellectual high ground frustrated that possibility almost from the beginning. John's reflex actions were dooming the team's efforts almost from each beginning.

It took a couple more sessions to come up with a system of flags that would warn John when he was behaving in this manner. Some of them were quite funny. If I was monitoring the meeting and he started down that road, I would take off my tie and toss it into the middle of the table. What was funnier – others quickly decoded the action and began the same behavior. One team member – who had never been known to actually wear a tie – began to wear one to the meetings. When asked about it he replied, "I have as much of a right to have my voice as anybody else."

~~~~~~~~~~

Consultants and Prudence

Lately I have been remembering fondly an old friend who lived in Jacksonville, Florida. When I first met him he was at the end of a long and wildly successful career in the real estate and railroad businesses. He used to have breakfast every Sunday morning at the old downtown Holiday Inn. He could afford to eat anywhere but he was a man of habits and that old restaurant suited him.

One particular Sunday I joined him for breakfast and we spent a couple of enjoyable hours talking about this and that. His wide range of interests and experiences – and active intellect – made him an interesting and stimulating breakfast partner. I remember that we discussed, among other things, the proper role of a board of directors, the value of an advisory board, the nature of leadership and leadership styles, spirituality, the value of mentoring and mentors as well as that of life mentoring. It was a very stimulating and wide-ranging session.

Things took a turn when I asked him about the proper use and role of consultants. He paused for a long time and then said, "Oh, I've had my experiences with consultants. At the beginning of every engagement, I'm the one with the money and they're the ones with the experience. If everything goes as they plan, by the end of the engagement they'll be the ones with the money and I'll have the experience."

We both laughed and then he got quiet again. "Chief," he said quietly "always remember that salesmen always sell what they have in inventory – whether you need it or not. Your job is to only buy what you need – what adds value."

When I pressed him on the subject he added "never accept the value that a salesman puts on his goods – and all consultants are essentially salesmen. Before you pay a consultant a dime you should have agreed on the value that will be added to your interests as a result of their work. And always remember, any good salesmen would rather make a killing than a contribution."

I've kept that lesson close – and I've been on both sides of the principal-consultant relationship. It seems to me the lesson is more useful now than then. Lots of salesmen are out there selling the latest and greatest fad – but few can make a direct connection to the bottom line of their client's business anymore – or, it seems, care to at all.

I've developed a couple of rules that seem to help.

- If the consultant is selling a concept run like hell

- If a consultant seems to feel that the details of your business are less important than the 'neat' aspects of their product or service, make sure that they pay the tab and then run like hell

- If a consultant will not tie their compensation to your results, smile and leave discretely

- If a consultant tells you that he understands your business better than you do, offer to sell it to him so that he can have a chance to prove it – but take cash

– no checks or IOUs

- If a consultant seems to be operating under the premise that he is smarter than you or that you are somehow out of step with the cutting edge of technology, signal for the waiter and have him escorted out of the restaurant.

Every principal who has needed to employ a consultant has developed their own set of rules. These are mine.

~~~~~~~~~~~

Change – Two of Many Perspectives

During my six tours as a CEO and through the years of working with other CEOs, I have developed an understanding of the process of change that is considerably different from the one I learned at the Sloan School. I find that helping CEOs understand the subtleties of change is one of the major contributions that I make to their future and the future of their companies. Although I do not see change dualistically, it may be helpful to describe two of the major approaches to change in the constellation.

Action That Creates Change: I see this first approach to change in modernist and primarily tactical terms. It is presumptuous. CEOs often style themselves as visionaries or in messianic terms. Their self-images are ego-focused; they proceed as actors – proactively driving change often over the resistance of the world as they find it and the people on their team.

There are times when envisioning change in this way can be very productive. Change focused on a clear understanding of the needs of an organization is a good example. This is a form of engineering – tactical and directed. An example might be a company that is poised to move to the next level.

There are other times when this envisioning of change can be destructive. Change based on a self-serving misunderstanding of an organization's need or a projection of bias onto those needs is a good example. This is a form of transference. An example might be the ego projection of a CEO onto a company. Here, the issues involved are inherently psychological.

Context That Creates Change: I see this second approach in post-modernist and strategic terms. It is inherently reactive. CEOs see themselves as pragmatists or in opportunistic terms. Their self-images are context-focused;

they proceed as reactors – co-actively managing change as they take advantage of the evolving business context and evolution of the people on their team.

CEOs that are good at dealing with this kind of context-driven-change have keen eyes and ears that are sensitive to trends within their space. Being able to pick up the 'thin edge of the change wedge' is such an important capability in a postmodernist world where change is the one constant. This is an exercise in highly sensitive perception.

The destructive side of this approach to change comes when context is overridden by a counter tendency. I have encountered CEOs that attempt to deal with rapidly changing context by rapidly changing their approach to managing their company. This amounts to moving the flatware around on the table. Each new period brings yet another 'visionaries vision'. The roiling waters of a CEO's capricious nature mask the evolution of context and limit potential.

Change Is: An effective approach to dealing with change involves considering these and other visions. It requires a constantly readjusted balance among them as developments demand. It is an extremely subtle dance. Difficulties in effectively addressing change come from not only the inherently complex nature of change and the human reaction to it – but also from ineffective understandings of the situation present. Simply put, approaching change from an egocentric perspective when contextual evolutions are driving the need to change is a kamikaze raid on a vacant lot. Alternatively, approaching change as a reaction to contextual evolutions when tactical responses are called for generates a similar result. Both are a waste of energy, resources and time.

~~~~~~~~~~

Parting Thoughts

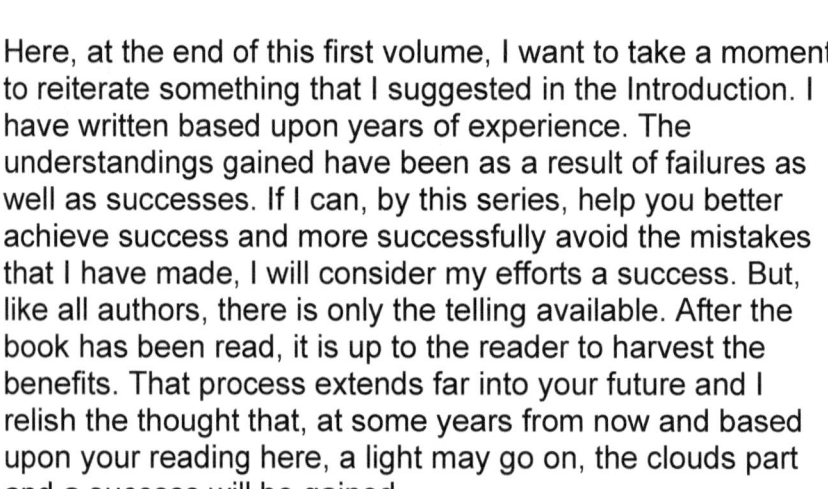

Here, at the end of this first volume, I want to take a moment to reiterate something that I suggested in the Introduction. I have written based upon years of experience. The understandings gained have been as a result of failures as well as successes. If I can, by this series, help you better achieve success and more successfully avoid the mistakes that I have made, I will consider my efforts a success. But, like all authors, there is only the telling available. After the book has been read, it is up to the reader to harvest the benefits. That process extends far into your future and I relish the thought that, at some years from now and based upon your reading here, a light may go on, the clouds part and a success will be gained.

The road to being a better CEO is inherently the same as the one which helps you be a better human being. There are plenty of places to learn about the techniques and technologies of business but, what will differentiate you as a rising star is your humanity.

I would leave you with one request. My journey is not yet finished and I am always eager to learn from others. If you care to take the time to tell me your stories, I assure you that you will find an interested ear and, just possibly, a place in the following volumes of this series.

With grateful thanks,
Dr. Earl R. Smith II
DrSmith@Dr-Smith.com

www.ingramcontent.com/pod-product-compliance
Lightning Source LLC
Chambersburg PA
CBHW051455170526
45166CB00001B/251